THE HIVE BEACH CAFÉ
COOKBOOK

DEDICATED TO BILL & JOAN

THANKS FOR THE PAST 50 YEARS, & PARTICULARLY FOR THE SUPPORT, GUIDANCE & MOTIVATION PROVIDED OVER THE LAST 20 YEARS IN BUSINESS TOGETHER

Recipes by Tim Attrill, Barry George, Tim Gibb and Giles Greening

Edited by Rufus Purdy

Photography by Graham Wiffen

FOREWORD

It's ironic I should be talking about my love of Dorset produce. I am a Londoner, born and bred, and my relationship with the place I now call home has evolved over many years. When I came to Dorset to set up my cookery school, I knew the county had one of Britain's best-stocked natural larders, but I wasn't sure how many cooks and chefs were around who cared enough to make the most of these fabulous local ingredients. When I first visited The Hive Beach Café in Burton Bradstock, though, I knew immediately I was in safe hands.

Steve Attrill – the man who has built The Hive up from a beach shack selling bacon sandwiches to the stylish seafood destination it is today – came over to say hello and, as he does with every new face who comes through the door, gave me the warmest of welcomes. Straightaway, I loved the informality of the place; the higgledy-piggeldy décor and the way the sea always remained in view through the canvas walls. And the location, nestled between towering Jurassic Coast cliffs and the water, was idyllic. The lobster I ordered was as fresh and delicious as any I've tasted, and I asked Steve where he sourced it. 'See that rock,' he said, pointing out of the window. 'About three feet to the left of that.'

Since that first visit, I've raved about The Hive to anyone who'll listen. Its intelligent approach to fish and seafood cookery – in which natural flavours are always allowed to shine through – makes it one of my favourite foodie destinations in the UK. I particularly admire its firm stance on sustainability, and its dedication to less-fashionable fish that don't threaten our dwindling stocks. The café buys direct from day boats who use line-catching methods, it gets its crabs and lobsters from the beach on its doorstep, and it's every bit as zealous about using Dorset produce as I am.

The talented team of chefs at The Hive (one of whom, I must admit, I recommended to the café) has never failed to impress me. And the recipes they've created for this book are a wonderful blend of the innovative and the inspiring. Divided into four seasons, they showcase what's fresh, available and at its absolute best at each point of the year. And, thanks to the QR-code included with each one, you can download favourites to your phone to make ingredient-sourcing all the easier. I hope you enjoy creating the dishes as much as I have.

Lesley Waters

CONTENTS

SPRING

20   Grilled herrings with horseradish crème fraîche

22   Langoustines with spring pea risotto

24   Turbot with baby leeks & cava cream sauce

26   The Hive ultimate fish burger

28   Seafood, tomato & chorizo broth

32   Razor clams with cider, leeks & parsley

34   Baked cod with a herb crust

36   Chargrilled mackerel with salsa verde

38   Seared salmon with buttered spinach

40   Monkfish in streaky bacon

42   John Dory with crispy leeks & mustard sauce

44   Scallops in a beurre noisette

48   Halibut with mussels & saffron cream sauce

50   Hive hash

52   Baked turbot steak with saffron aïoli

54   Roasted hake with sautéed spring greens

56   Grey mullet with crab and Jersey royal salad

58   Lesley Waters' hot & sour prawn soup

60   Sea trout with curly kale bubble & squeak

64   Smoked haddock with asparagus benedict

66   Scallop scampi with homemade tartare sauce

68   Smoked mackerel with horseradish crème fraîche

70   John Dory in a cockle, baby leek & cider broth

72   Sardines on toast Neapolitan

74   Spiced spider crab gratin

SUMMER

78 Baked John Dory with rosemary & cherry tomatoes

80 The Hive cold shellfish platter

82 Plaice goujons with minted mushy peas

84 Roasted gurnard with olive oil & sea salt

86 Lemon sole with anchovy & herb butter

88 Mackerel with red onion & red pepper salsa

90 Mussels with white wine, herbs, garlic & cream

94 Weymouth crab & avocado salad

96 Hake with chilli & tomato chutney

98 Chargrilled black bream with lemon & rosemary

100 Dover sole in parsley & garlic butter

102 Tempura cod with minted mushy peas

104 Grilled lobster with garlic butter

106 Seabass for two

110 Seared scallops with pancetta & chorizo

112 Baked dabs with lemon & garlic butter

114 Smoked salmon & scrambled eggs

116 Seabass Niçoise

118 Squid with a chilli, coriander & lime butter

122 Burton Bradstock brown crab salad

124 Skate wing with brown butter & caper sauce

126 Huss fishfingers with homemade tartare sauce

128 Baked plaice with crayfish & herb butter

130 Lesley Waters' glazed lemon sole tart

132 Peppered sardines with sea salt

104

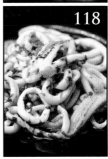

118

88

CONTENTS

AUTUMN

136 Dover sole with a shrimp & caper butter

138 Oysters Rockefeller

140 Brill with sautéed wild mushrooms

142 Surf clam chowder

144 Tempura herring roe salad

148 Scallops with boudin noir & pea purée

150 Crevette prawns in a sweet & sticky chilli sauce

152 Homecured gravlax

154 Lobster bisque

156 Pan-fried huss with Chinese five spice

158 Mussels in a red wine, thyme & tomato sauce

160 Mackerel with new potatoes & tapenade

164 Baked halibut steaks with a hazelnut crust

166 Cuttlefish stew

168 Smoked haddock rarebit with roasted tomatoes

170 Red mullet with homemade pesto

172 Chilli crab linguine

174 Lesley Waters' rainbow trout fishcakes

176 Turbot with blackeyed bean cassoulet

180 Razor clams with a lemon & lime vinaigrette

182 Smoked haddock chowder

184 Kippers & soft poached eggs on granary toast

186 Oysters & Guinness

188 Tempura brill with a creamy pancetta sauce

190 Grilled garfish with lemon zest, parsley & olive oil

WINTER

194 Hot shellfish risotto

196 Baked pouting in a curried mussel broth

198 Whiting goujons with guacamole & chilli salt

200 The Hive fish pie

202 Roasted cod with buttered cabbage, pancetta & tomato

204 Baked scallops in a cheese sauce

206 Brill with a poached duck's egg & crispy pancetta

210 The Hive hot shellfish platter

212 Smoked haddock kedgeree

214 Lesley Waters' garlic mussel bisque

216 The Hive breakfast bap

218 Roast pollock in a shellfish stew

222 Seafood soup

224 Roasted turbot steak in a wild mushroom sauce

226 Oysters three ways

228 Smoked haddock risotto fishcakes

230 Scallops in a creamy leek & saffron sauce

232 Salmon & wild mushrooms in a puff pastry parcel

236 Mussels in a red Thai broth

238 Tempura pollock in a creamy leek & saffron sauce

240 Lobster thermidor

242 Bouillabaisse

244 Mackerel fillets with celeriac remoulade

246 Crispy salt & pepper squid

248 Oysters with pancetta & creamy parmesan sauce

HOW TO
USE THIS BOOK

A NOTE ON THE RECIPES

All the recipes in this book have been chosen to take advantage of produce that's at its best and readily available during its designated season. The fish, seafood and shellfish we use at The Hive are delivered to us daily by our network of local suppliers but, so long as you use fresh, locally sourced ingredients, your creations should taste every bit as good as ours. There's an ingredient list with each recipe, but we haven't included salt and pepper on this, as we've assumed everyone will have this basic seasoning to hand. At The Hive, we use Cornish sea salt and freshly ground black pepper to provide that extra boost of flavour, and we'd recommend you do the same. Other ingredients worth keeping in your cupboard include butter, free-range eggs, unwaxed lemons and fresh garlic. Make sure you've got some extra-virgin olive oil and a few tins of good-quality chopped tomatoes, too.

QR-CODES

Each of the QR-codes in this book – the crossword-like squares that appear alongside the food pictures – provides access to a website from which you can download jpeg or pdf versions of each recipe. This allows you to store all the details on an iPhone or other Smartphone, and have the ingredient list to hand. Downloading the information to your phone is simple…

● Most Smartphones come with a QR-code reader. If you don't have a QR-code reader on your Smartphone, go to your App store to download one. We recommend i-nigma.
● Once you've downloaded the QR-code reader, launch it as you would any other App. If you can't find it in your Apps folder, then look in your phone's Downloads folder.
● Your phone's camera will automatically start looking for a QR-code to scan, so line it up over the one that accompanies the recipe you want to prepare.
● Your phone will then scan the QR-code and take you directly to the recipe webpage. Click either the pdf or jpeg file, and the information will be downloaded to your Photo Gallery or Downloads folder. You will then be able to access and enlarge these files at any time.
● iPhone users should select the jpeg option. Once the file has opened, simply tap the screen and you will be presented with an option to save it to the Camera Roll in your Photos folder.

HOW TO PREPARE FISH

ENSURING YOUR FISH IS FRESH

- Are the eyes clear? Avoid any fish that has cloudy, dull-looking eyes.
- Is the skin firm and shiny? If it's soft to the touch, then move on.
- Are the gills red and clear? Don't touch anything with cloudy slime around this area.
- Is it odourless? If the fish has a strong smell, then it's past its best.
- Does the fish feel wet and is its clear, slimy protective covering still evident? Avoid if not.

CHECKING YOUR FISH IS COOKED

- If you are cooking a whole fish – or an unfilleted portion – you can tell whether or not it's ready by inserting a small knife into the section nearest the bones, and checking the flesh has changed from a translucent colour to a more solid (usually white) one.

- If you're using fillets (ie, bone-free portions) of fish, there are two ways to check whether they're ready to eat. The first is to insert a small knife into the flesh at the centre of the fillet and look to see whether it has changed from a translucent colour to a more solid one. The second – which we recommend for thicker fillets – is to insert a knife into the centre, then withdraw it and place it flat on the back of your hand. If the knife is hot, the fillet will be cooked.

HOW TO PREPARE FISH

FILLETING, SCALING & PIN-BONING

● Filleting refers to removing the main part of the skeleton, leaving you with a portion of fish that's relatively bone-free. Pin-boning refers to the more intricate job of removing any bones that are left after filleting.
● When filleting, make sure you use a sharp knife; and always direct the knife away from you as this will avert injury should it slip.
● Scaling refers to the messy task of scraping away the fish's scales with a knife. This is done from tail to head, working against the grain of the scales. We recommend using a palette knife when scaling, as – thanks to its blunt edges – it's unlikely to break the skin. At The Hive, we also use scallop shells, which work surprisingly well.

FILLETING A FLATFISH

● With a sharp filleting knife, cut along the sides of the fish's head down to the bone.
● Cut along the back of the fish, from head to tail, following the line of the fish's slightly raised backbone.
● Carefully cut the flesh away from each side of the backbone, keeping your knife flat and as close to the bones as possible. Fold the flesh back as you do so. This will produce two fillets.
● Turn the fish over and repeat the process on the other side.

FILLETING A ROUNDFISH

● Scale the fish with a knife or scallop shell. Carefully scrape from the tail towards the head to remove scales, but be careful not to break the skin. Repeat the process on the other side.
● With a sharp filleting knife, cut around the fish's head down to the bone.
● Cut back into the fish, following the spine-line, and carefully remove the fillet from the bone. Fold the flesh back as you work your way along the fish. This will produce one fillet.
● Remove any bones that are left and trim the fillet.
● Turn the fish over and repeat the process on the other side.

HOW TO
PREPARE SEAFOOD
& SHELLFISH

SQUID

- Take the squid's head in one hand and the body in the other, and gently pull. The head, along with the intestines, should come away easily. Cut the tentacles from the head.
- Squeeze the beak out from the middle of the tentacles, and discard it.
- Insert your hand into the body pouch and pull out the plasticky quill and any roe.
- Pull the two fins from either side of the body pouch, then pull off the translucent skin.
- Rinse the pouch thoroughly with cold water.

CRAB

- Bring a pan of salted water up to the boil.
- Kill your crab by first inserting a skewer between its eyes. Then turn it over and push a skewer into the small pointed flap towards the back of its shell. Give the skewer a sharp tap, so that you feel it hit the other side of the shell.
- Place the crab in the boiling water for 10 minutes, then turn off the heat and allow it to cool in the water.
- Once the crab has cooled, take it out from the pan, and remove and discard the grey, feathery gills (known as dead man's fingers) from the underside of the body.

LOBSTER

- Place your lobster into the freezer for 2 hours before you need it.
- When you're ready to start cooking, bring a pan of salted water up to the boil and add the lobster straight from the freezer. Boil it for 10 minutes then allow it to cool in the water.
- Cut the lobster in half lengthways with a sharp knife. Remove the dark intestinal tract that runs down the middle, then get rid of the green-coloured liver and any roe.
- Use a hammer or nutcrackers to break the hard shell of the claws and access the meat.

MUSSELS & CLAMS

● When buying mussels or clams, make sure that they are still alive. Discard any that are open and do not close when tapped, and get rid of ones with shells that are cracked or damaged.
● Rinse your mussels or clams in cold water to remove any dirt.
● Use a knife to scrape off any barnacles or persistent dirt from the shells.
● Pull out any beards – the fibrous strands that protrude from the shells – and rinse once more in cold running water. They are now ready to cook.

OYSTERS

● When buying oysters, make sure that they are still alive. They should feel heavy – live oysters carry a lot of water. Discard any that are open and do not close when tapped, and get rid of ones with shells that are cracked or damaged.
● Shucking – ie, opening – an oyster can be dangerous. At The Hive, we always place a tea towel over the hand in which we hold the oyster to prevent injury should the knife slip.
● Hold an oyster with the flatter side facing upwards, then take an oyster knife and push it into the hinge – the narrowest point – of the oyster. Be careful not to push too hard or the knife might slip.
● Twist the knife and lift off the top of the oyster shell. Remove this – taking care not to let any fragments fall into the bottom half – and free the oyster, which will be attached by a muscle to the shell.
● An oyster that is good to eat will smell clean and fresh when you open it. The liquid inside the shell should be clear rather than cloudy.

SCALLOPS

● When buying scallops, try to source hand-dived ones rather than the more common dredged variety. They are much cleaner, as well as being more environmentally friendly.
● Rinse your scallops in cold running water to get rid of any dirt.
● Gently ease open the scallop shell with a knife or other flat blade.
● Carefully slide the blade between the scallop and the top half of the shell, and cut through the piece of ligament that attaches the two.
● Repeat this process with the bottom half of the shell.
● Remove the unappetising black stomach sac, as well as any dirt and 'skirt', from the scallop, leaving just the white flesh and coral intact. It is now ready to cook.

HOW TO MAKE STOCK

FISH STOCK

INGREDIENTS

Butter

Olive oil

2 onions, sliced

1 stick celery, chopped

1 leek, sliced

1 fennel bulb, sliced

1kg fish bones (flatfish bones work best)

Glass white wine

2 bay leaves

6 black peppercorns

Sprig thyme

Small bunch parsley, chopped

● Melt a knob of butter and a drizzle of olive oil in a large saucepan, and sweat the onions until soft. Add the celery, leek and fennel, and cook for another couple of minutes.

● Add the fish bones and white wine, and cook until the liquid has reduced by half. Put in the bay leaves, peppercorns, thyme and parsley, and cover with water. Bring up to a gentle simmer and cook for 20 minutes, skimming regularly.

● Strain through a muslin-lined sieve. The fish stock is now ready to use.

SHELLFISH STOCK

INGREDIENTS

1kg shellfish shells

Butter

Olive oil

2 onions, sliced

1 stick celery, chopped

1 leek, sliced

2 tsp tomato purée

Glass white wine

1 star anise

2 bay leaves

6 black peppercorns

Small bunch parsley stalks

Sprig thyme

● Roast the shellfish shells in a hot oven until crisp and golden.

● Melt a knob of butter and a drizzle of olive oil in a large saucepan, and sweat the onions until soft. Add the celery and leek, and cook for another couple of minutes.

● Add the shellfish shells and tomato purée, and cook for 2 minutes. Then pour in the white wine and cook until the liquid has reduced by half.

● Add the star anise, bay leaves, peppercorns, parsley stalks and thyme to the pan, and cover with water. Bring up to a gentle simmer and cook for 30 minutes, skimming regularly.

● Strain the liquid through a muslin-lined sieve. The shellfish stock is now ready to use.

HOW TO MAKE SAUCES & ACCOMPANIMENTS

HOLLANDAISE SAUCE

INGREDIENTS

½ shallot, finely diced

100ml white wine

75ml white wine vinegar

1 bay leaf

250g butter

2 egg yolks

- Place the shallot, white wine, white wine vinegar, bay leaf and some freshly ground black pepper into a sauté pan, and bring to the boil.
- Simmer until the liquid has reduced by three-quarters, then strain it through a sieve and set aside in a warm place.
- Melt the butter in a small pan and allow it to boil for around 1 minute, until the fats separate. Let it cool for 1 minute or so, until the butter fat sinks to the bottom, then set aside.
- Pour the egg yolks into a mixing bowl, then add the reduced, sieved wine liquid. Blend together with a hand blender, then slowly pour in the clear, clarified butter (not the milky butter fat) while blending continually. Be careful not to pour too fast, otherwise the sauce will split.
- Stop adding the clarified butter when the sauce reaches a thick consistency.

MAYONNAISE

INGREDIENTS

2 egg yolks

2 tsp white wine vinegar

1 tsp Dijon mustard

300ml rapeseed oil

- Place the egg yolks, white wine vinegar and Dijon mustard into a food processor, along with sea salt and freshly ground black pepper, and blend until pale and creamy.
- Pour in the rapeseed oil in a steady stream, blending continually, until the mayonnaise reaches a thick consistency.

ROUILLE

INGREDIENTS

1 red pepper, cut in half and seeds removed
1 slice white bread
1 red chilli
1 egg yolk
300ml olive oil

● Preheat a grill and place the red pepper halves, skin side up, on a baking tray. Grill for a few minutes, until the skin has blackened and started to bubble, then remove.
● Once the red pepper has cooled, take off the skin.
● Place the skinned red pepper, white bread, chilli and egg yolk into a food processor, and blend until combined.
● Slowly pour in the olive oil, blending continually, until the sauce has reached a thick, creamy consistency.

ROCKET SALSA VERDE

INGREDIENTS

50g wild rocket
½ bunch basil, roughly torn
1 tbsp baby capers
1 tsp wholegrain mustard
4 tbsp extra-virgin olive oil
2 tbsp water

● Roughly chop the rocket and place it in a blender with the basil, baby capers, wholegrain mustard, olive oil and water.
● Blend until smooth and season well with sea salt and freshly ground black pepper.

TARTARE SAUCE

INGREDIENTS

100ml mayonnaise (see opposite)
Small handful pickled gherkins, chopped
Small handful pickled capers, chopped
Bunch flat-leaf parsley, chopped
½ red onion, finely diced
1 lemon, juiced

● Place the mayonnaise in a mixing bowl, then add the gherkins, capers, parsley, red onion and lemon juice. Mix well.
● Season with sea salt and freshly ground black pepper, then set aside in the fridge.

SPRING

GRILLED HERRINGS WITH HORSERADISH CRÈME FRAÎCHE

SERVES 2

A staple of Scandinavian cuisine, the humble herring has fallen out of fashion in the UK over the past few decades, despite it swimming around our coastline in huge numbers. But recent research shows that eating this fish, which is rich in Omega 3 oils, provides even more health benefits than originally thought. It helps that it tastes pretty marvellous, too. And this recipe, which matches its strong, unique flavour to the equally feisty ones of mustard and horseradish, gives it the perfect platform. Eat up; it's good for you…

INGREDIENTS

4 200–250g herrings, gutted, scaled and roes removed
Olive oil
100ml crème fraîche

1 tsp wholegrain mustard
1 tsp creamed horseradish
Small handful chives, finely chopped

● Preheat a hot grill. Place the herrings onto an oiled and seasoned baking tray, and sprinkle liberally with sea salt and freshly ground black pepper. Grill for around 7 minutes, until cooked through.
● Put the crème fraîche, mustard and horseradish into a bowl, and mix together. Feel free to add more horseradish if you like a slightly more aggressive sauce.
● Divide the herrings between 2 plates and spoon the crème fraîche mixture over the top so it melts on the warm fish. Sprinkle with chives and serve immediately with a watercress salad.

LANGOUSTINES WITH SPRING PEA RISOTTO

SERVES 2

This is a great risotto recipe for anyone put off by the stodgy, grey concoctions served up in cheap neighbourhood Italians. The lively flavours in the herb butter and sweetness of the garden peas work wonderfully with the succulent white meat in the langoustines to create a meal that zings as much with colour as it does with taste.

INGREDIENTS

2–3 large cups fish stock (see page 15)
200g butter
Handful fresh parsley, chopped
Handful fresh basil, chopped
Handful fresh mint, chopped
2 garlic cloves, finely diced
1 lemon, juiced and zested

12–16 langoustines, cut in half lengthways
1 shallot, diced
1 large cup Arborio rice
Glass white wine
Handful frozen peas
50–100ml double cream

● Preheat a hot grill and ensure your fish stock is simmering gently in a saucepan.
● Put three-quarters of the butter into a mixing bowl with the parsley, basil, mint, garlic, lemon juice and zest, and season with sea salt and freshly ground black pepper. Mix well.
● Arrange the langoustines, open side up, on a baking tray, and spread liberally with the herb butter. Set aside.
● Melt the remaining butter in a sauté pan and add the shallot. Cook for around 10 minutes over a low heat until it has softened without colouring. Add the Arborio rice and sauté for 1 minute, taking care not to burn the grains.
● Increase the heat to medium and pour in the wine. Simmer until the rice has absorbed all the liquid – again, ensuring you don't let it burn – then add a ladleful of fish stock. Stir until the rice has absorbed all the liquid then continue adding the stock in stages, stirring regularly and waiting until the rice has fully absorbed it before adding more.
● The risotto will be ready when the rice retains just a touch of bite. When you are 5 minutes from this point, add in the peas and place the langoustines under the hot grill for 2–4 minutes.
● Once the risotto is ready, pour in the cream. Warm it though and remove from the heat.
● Divide the risotto between 2 plates and arrange the langoustines on top in a wigwam fashion. Pour over any remaining herb butter and serve immediately with a wedge of lemon.

TURBOT WITH BABY LEEKS & CAVA CREAM SAUCE

SERVES 2

Known as King of the Flatfish, the turbot is famed for its rich taste and subtle texture. Luckily, throughout the spring months, its kingdom seems to be Dorset's Chesil Bank and the Race off Portland; and local fisherman Brett Hibbitt regularly brings us fish of 10 kilos or more. In this recipe, the tender baby leeks in the delicate and classy sauce enhance the flavour of the firm, white flesh without overpowering it. The turbot undoubtedly likes to be the star of the show, so let him.

INGREDIENTS

10 baby leeks
Butter
1 shallot, finely diced
125ml cava

100ml fish stock (see page 15)
50–100ml double cream
400–500g turbot fillet, skin left on
Olive oil

● Preheat your oven to 220°C/425°F. Blanch the baby leeks in salted boiling water for 2–3 minutes, then remove and place in cold water to cool and stop them from cooking further. Drain and set aside.

● To make the sauce, melt a knob of butter in a sauté pan and sweat the shallot for a couple of minutes, then add the cava and fish stock, and reduce by three-quarters. Pour in the cream and bring to the boil, then remove from the heat and set aside in a warm place. If you prefer a smooth sauce, pass it through a sieve at this point.

● Preheat a griddle pan. Place the turbot fillet, skin side up, onto an oiled and seasoned roasting tray. Season the fish and drizzle with olive oil, then roast for 10–15 minutes, until cooked through.

● While the fish is cooking, chargrill the leeks in the griddle pan, turning occasionally, until they are charred on all sides. This should take around 2–3 minutes.

● To serve, pour some sauce onto a large plate, arrange the leeks over it and place the fish on top.

THE HIVE ULTIMATE FISH BURGER

SERVES 2

The fishfinger sandwich has always been a favourite late-night snack for the time-pressed cook in search of something comforting to eat, but the fish burger – despite being every bit as moreish and taking no longer to prepare – rarely gets a look-in. We at The Hive are on a mission to change that. Our Ultimate Fish Burger uses the finest, freshest cod in a light, crispy tempura batter, and is served with a homemade sauce that is a million times better than anything that comes in a jar.

INGREDIENTS

3 cups plain flour

150ml sparkling water

Sunflower oil, for deep-frying

2 200–225g cod fillets, scaled and pin-boned

2 large soft white burger buns

Iceberg lettuce

Homemade tartare sauce (see page 17)

- Whisk together 2 cups of flour with the sparkling water to create a thin batter. Set aside.
- Preheat the sunflower oil to 180°C/350°F in a large pan or deep-fat fryer. Spread out the remaining flour and plenty of sea salt on a baking tray, and coat the cod fillet thoroughly with the mixture.
- Dip the floured fillets into the batter and place in the hot oil, skin side down. Deep-fry for around 4–6 minutes, until the batter is golden and the fish is cooked through. Remove and place on a piece of kitchen paper to absorb the excess oil.
- While the fish is cooking, cut the burger buns in half and arrange the lettuce and homemade tartare sauce on the top section. Place the fish on the bottom section and put the other half on top.
- Serve immediately with chips or sauté potatoes.

SEAFOOD, TOMATO & CHORIZO BROTH

SERVES 2

This dish evolved from our famous winter seafood soup and, like its cold-weather cousin, is packed with flavour and warmth. It's the ideal meal to sit down to after a bracing beach walk in which you've been battered by squally winds and spring showers.

INGREDIENTS

12–16 mussels

2 raw chorizo, sliced thinly

2 slices pancetta, finely chopped

½ leek, finely sliced

½ onion, finely diced

2 sticks celery, finely diced

Pinch smoked paprika

Pinch cayenne pepper

440g good-quality tinned chopped tomatoes

300ml fish stock (see page 15)

440g tinned butter beans, drained

Butter

2 garlic cloves, finely diced

6 king prawns

150g squid tubes, cleaned and cut into rings

50–100g white fish (cod, haddock, coley, etc), cut into small cubes

2 tbsp crème fraîche

Handful flat-leaf parsley, chopped

● Wash the mussels in cold water and discard any that do not close when tapped.

● Fry the chorizo and pancetta in a non-stick saucepan over a medium heat for 1–2 minutes, until they start to exude fat. Add the leek, onion, celery, smoked paprika and cayenne pepper, and sweat for 5–7 minutes until soft.

● Pour in the tomatoes and fish stock, and season with sea salt and freshly ground black pepper. Simmer for 5 minutes, then add the butter beans and simmer for another 10 minutes until the liquid has reduced slightly.

● Melt a knob of butter in a hot frying pan then cook the garlic and king prawns for 2–3 minutes. Add the mussels, cover and toss, then – when they start to open – tip in the squid rings and fry for 1 minute. Pour the fried seafood mixture and its juices into the tomato broth, and add the white fish. Cook for 2 minutes.

● Divide the seafood between 2 plates and pour the remaining broth over the top. Finish with a spoonful of crème fraîche and a sprinkling of flat-leaf parsley; serve with crusty granary bread.

RAZOR CLAMS WITH CIDER, LEEKS & PARSLEY

SERVES 2

Named after their resemblance to the cutthroat razors favoured by Sweeney Todd-era barbers, razor clams have a similar texture to squid and a sweet, scallop-like taste. We get ours up from Poole Harbour or Studland Bay – taking only the ones that poke from the sand and wriggle when moved – and wrap them up in a damp tea towel, which we keep at the bottom of our fridge. Cold water would kill them and only super-fresh razor clams are worth eating. This recipe, which teams their gentle flavour with the more robust ones of appley cider, peppery leeks and fresh, grassy parsley, is a great showcase for their talents.

INGREDIENTS

Butter

2 garlic cloves, finely chopped

1 leek, finely shredded

12–14 fresh razor clams, rinsed

1 large glass cider

100ml double cream

Handful parsley, chopped

- Get two serving bowls ready – this dish takes only a few minutes to prepare.
- Melt a knob of butter in a large saucepan over a high heat, and sweat the garlic and leek until soft.
- Add the razor clams and toss in the garlic-and-leek butter. Pour in the cider and immediately cover the pan.
- Steam the clams for 1–2 minutes then take off the lid and add the cream. Bring to the boil and simmer for 1 minute.
- Divide the razor clams between the 2 serving dishes (don't pour over the rest of the sauce as this can often contain grit from the shellfish), sprinkle with parsley and serve immediately with a hunk of crusty bread.

BAKED COD WITH A HERB CRUST

SERVES 2

A crispy coating on fish provides an extra element of texture. And when that coating is packed with spring herbs and lemon zest, a whole new taste platform is created. In this recipe, the firm, flakiness of cod is lifted totally by the freshness and zing of the crust, and this most everyday of fish is elevated to something truly special. Feel free to substitute the cod for haddock, coley, pollock or halibut; all will benefit from this delicious topping.

INGREDIENTS

2 250g cod fillets, scaled and pin-boned

Olive oil

3–4 slices white bread

Small handful parsley or basil, chopped

25g butter, melted

1 lemon, juiced and zested

1 shallot, diced

1 bay leaf

6 peppercorns

Glass white wine

½ glass white wine vinegar

100g butter, cubed

2 handfuls salad leaves

● Preheat your oven to 220°C/425°F. Place the cod fillets, skin side down, onto an oiled and seasoned baking tray.

● Put the bread into a food processor and blitz. Add the herbs, melted butter, lemon zest, sea salt and black pepper, and blitz briefly once again.

● Sprinkle the mixture liberally over the cod fillets, then bake for around 10 minutes, until cooked through.

● While the fish is cooking, put the shallot, bay leaf, peppercorns, lemon juice, white wine and white wine vinegar into a saucepan, and reduce until just enough liquid remains to cover the bottom of the pan. Remove from the heat.

● Whisk in the butter, a couple of cubes at a time. When the sauce reaches a thick, glossy consistency, set it aside in a warm (not hot) place.

● Arrange a few salad leaves on 2 plates, pour a small amount of sauce around these and place the cod fillets on top. Serve immediately, garnished with lemon.

CHARGRILLED MACKEREL WITH SALSA VERDE

SERVES 2

Mackerel are plentiful off the Dorset coast throughout spring and summer. Indeed, if you were to walk from West Bay in the east to Chesil Cove in the west, you would see fishermen hauling them in all along the route. The small 'joeys' caught at the start of the season and the much fatter specimens brought in towards the end feed everyone from beach-barbecuers to eager customers at The Hive, and their delicious oily flavour is guaranteed to send everyone home happy. We've found that sharp salsa verde and aromatic lemon oil make great accompaniments.

INGREDIENTS

2 lemons

Good-quality olive oil

4 medium-sized mackerel, gutted and scaled

Homemade rocket salsa verde (see page 17)

Crusty bread, to serve

● Cut 1 lemon into six wedges, then arrange the pieces on a lipped baking tray. Drizzle with 300ml olive oil and cook in the oven for around 2 hours at a low heat, until the lemon is caramelised but not burnt. Once cooked, strain the excess oil into a jug and set aside.

● Preheat a griddle pan over a high heat. Place the mackerel onto the hot griddle and do not move for at least 3–4 minutes. Turn over and repeat on the other side.

● Divide the mackerel between 2 dishes, and drizzle the homemade rocket salsa verde and lemon oil on top. Serve immediately with lemon wedges and crusty bread.

SEARED SALMON WITH BUTTERED SPINACH

SERVES 2

As well as looking and tasting fabulous, this dish is a nutritionist's dream. The Omega 3 oils in the salmon, and the vitamins and iron in the antioxidant-rich spinach do all sorts of good things to your body while the delicious combination of flavours sends your tastebuds into overdrive. Here at The Hive, we've found it's key to get the salmon skin as crisp as possible, as this adds an extra dimension of texture that makes an otherwise simple recipe taste seriously stunning.

INGREDIENTS

400–500g skin-on salmon fillet, scaled and pin-boned

Olive oil

Butter

150g baby spinach, washed

● Preheat your oven to 220°C/425°F. Preheat a non-stick frying pan until smoking-hot.

● Divide the salmon fillet into 2 portions. Season each section and drizzle with olive oil, paying particular attention to the skin. Place the fillets, skin side down, in the pan. Let them cook for 2–3 minutes without moving – this gives the skin time to crisp.

● Remove the salmon fillets and place them, skin side up, onto an oiled and seasoned baking tray. Bake in the oven for 4–5 minutes. Salmon can be served slightly rare if you prefer; the meat turns light-pink when thoroughly cooked.

● While the fish is cooking, melt a knob of butter in the frying pan you used for the salmon then add the spinach, and season with sea salt and freshly ground black pepper. Sauté until wilted.

● Divide the spinach between 2 plates and arrange the salmon fillets on top. Serve immediately with new potatoes.

MONKFISH IN STREAKY BACON

SERVES 2

This is a great dish for the beginning of the barbecue season – though it can also be cooked on the grill, the griddle or in the oven – as the firm, sturdy flesh of monkfish is able to soak up strong flavours in a similar way to meat. We always use rashers of Dorset Denhay bacon when making this recipe, as its saltiness works wonderfully with the succulent taste of the monkfish, but any good-quality streaky bacon will do. Feel free to vary what's included on the kebabs, too; we've only listed our favourite combination as a guide.

INGREDIENTS

400g monkfish tail, cut into 3cm cubes
8–10 rashers streaky bacon, cut in half
16 cherry tomatoes
2 garlic cloves, finely chopped
Small handful parsley, finely chopped

50g butter
Olive oil
2 handfuls salad leaves
1 lemon, cut into wedges

● Wrap the monkfish cubes in the streaky bacon and thread them onto 4 wooden barbecue skewers, placing a cherry tomato in between each piece of fish. Arrange 4 wrapped monkfish cubes onto each skewer.

● Add the garlic and a pinch of parsley to the butter, and mix together. Rub some of this mixture onto the monkfish and cherry tomato skewers, and set aside in the fridge.

● Heat a barbecue, grill or griddle, or preheat your oven to 220°C/425°F.

● If you're barbecuing or griddling, spray a little oil onto the cooking surface and place the kebabs on top. If you're cooking the kebabs in the oven or under the grill, place the skewers onto an oiled baking tray before cooking. All methods require 6–8 minutes cooking time; baste with garlic butter every couple of minutes to ensure the kebabs stay moist.

● Serve immediately with dressed salad leaves, lemon wedges and a drizzle of cooking juices over the top.

JOHN DORY WITH CRISPY LEEKS & MUSTARD SAUCE

SERVES 2

Though John Dory are more plentiful during the summer months, they start to appear on fishmongers' ice counters as early as March or April. And their delicate, sweet taste is a perfect match for peppery spring leeks and buttered new potatoes. For this recipe, you need a fish that's as fresh as possible, so look out for ones with shiny, bulging eyes and skin that has a clean, wet sheen. It should have a faint, pleasant aroma of the sea rather than a strong fishy smell, which indicates it's been out of the water a little too long.

INGREDIENTS

500g John Dory, filleted and pin-boned
Olive oil
Butter
1 shallot, diced

100ml fish stock (see page 15)
100ml double cream
1 tsp wholegrain mustard
1 leek, julienned into 3cm strips

● Preheat a hot grill. Place the John Dory fillets, skin side up, onto an oiled and seasoned baking tray. Season the fish and drizzle with olive oil, then grill for 6–7 minutes, until cooked through.

● Put a knob of butter into a sauté pan then sweat the shallot over a moderate heat for 1 minute. Pour in the fish stock and reduce by half then add the cream and mustard, and reduce by half again. Set aside in a warm place.

● Heat a splash of olive oil in a small frying pan until it is very hot but not smoking. Add the leek strips and fry for 1–2 minutes, until crisp and golden. Remove and place on a piece of kitchen paper to soak up any excess oil. Season with a little sea salt.

● Divide the sauce between 2 prewarmed plates, stack the John Dory fillets on top and finish with the crispy leeks. Serve immediately with new potatoes or chips.

SCALLOPS IN A BEURRE NOISETTE

SERVES 2

Beurre noisette – a French expression that translates as hazelnut butter – is something of a misnomer; the recipe includes no hazelnuts and instead gets its name from the nutty taste and colour that butter takes on when cooked with lemon juice and capers. These acidic ingredients not only cut through the richness of the butter, but help prevent it from burning and becoming beurre noir. This simple sauce, made solely with store-cupboard essentials, is usually served with skate wing, but it works wonderfully with scallops, too. Make sure you pre-read the recipe and have all the ingredients to hand. Everything happens very quickly with this one.

INGREDIENTS

Olive oil

12–16 scallops depending on size

Butter

½ lemon, juiced

1 tbsp capers (baby capers are best)

Handful parsley, chopped

● Preheat a non-stick sauté pan until it is smoking-hot. Oil and season the scallops, and arrange them in the pan in a clockwise direction, remembering your starting point. After around 90 seconds, turn the scallops over in the same order.

● Reduce the heat to low and cook the scallops for another 90 seconds. Then remove in the same order as you put them into the pan to ensure they're evenly cooked. Divide between two prewarmed plates and set aside in a warm place.

● Put a generous knob of butter into the same pan and allow it to separate into milk solids and butter fats as it melts. When the milk solids start to turn golden-brown after around 2 minutes, add the lemon juice, capers and parsley, then remove from the heat.

● Spoon a small amount of the beurre noisette over the scallops and serve immediately with hunks of crusty bread.

OUR SUPPLIERS: SAMWAYS, BRIDPORT

'We date back 50 years as a company,' says Clive Samways (*right*), managing director of Samways fish merchants and international transporters. 'My father worked in Bridport, and in his spare time he used to go fishing and sell his catch from a little wooden barrow on the quayside at West Bay. Now the company has grown to cover the whole of the south coast – from Rye right through to Porstmouth – and we have parts of our infrastructure in place in all the major ports. We have stalls in Newlyn, Brixham and Looe, and we have full-time Samways individuals working there, landing the fish, speaking to the boats, knowing the skippers.

'We deal with everyone from major supermarkets to local restaurants and, of course, The Hive, who we've known for years – they're real Dorset people. And, though we even sell to retailers in mainland Europe, we like to keep a local presence. We do all the markets – Sturminster, Castle Cary, Sherborne, Bridport – and we've got a retail shop in West Bay, which is normally open seven days a week. As you can imagine, the summer trade there is phenomenal. Pots of cockles, dressed crabs…

'This is very much a family business. My wife Sarah (*left*) looks after the catering side; her father runs our retail arm. We've got our son Lance working for us as well, and there's Charlie and Jess in the next generation. So we've got more family, more blood coming through as the company grows and expands. We've got plans to extend and improve our facilities here in Bridport to be the best equipped in the south of England. And that, we hope, will create a lot of local jobs. It's our dream that everyone should be able to get their fish within 24 hours of it being caught.'

Samways, Gore Cross Business Park, Bridport (01308 422201; www.samwaysfish.com).

HALIBUT WITH MUSSELS & SAFFRON CREAM SAUCE

SERVES 2

The largest of the flatfish that we use here at The Hive, the halibut is certainly an impressive beast. We regularly get fish that weigh more than 50 kilos, and some are closer to 80. One 75 kilo fish that arrived recently fed 160 people. This recipe, which teams its firm, clean-tasting meat with creamy, delicately spiced mussels, deals in far more manageable portions.

INGREDIENTS

200ml fish stock (see page 15)

150ml double cream

Pinch saffron strands

1 bay leaf

Thai Nam Pla fish sauce (optional)

12–16 mussels

2 350-400g halibut steaks

Olive oil

Butter

⅓ leek, finely sliced

Glass white wine

Handful chives, chopped

● First, prepare the saffron cream sauce. Put the fish stock, cream, saffron and bay leaf into a saucepan and bring to a gentle boil. Cook until the liquid has reduced by between a half and two-thirds, and the sauce has taken on the golden-yellow colour of the saffron. Season to taste and – if you like – add a couple of drops of Thai Nam Pla fish sauce. Set aside in a warm place.

● Wash the mussels in cold water and discard any that do not close when tapped.

● Preheat your oven to 220°C/425°F. Place the halibut steaks onto an oiled roasting tray. Season the fish and drizzle with olive oil, then roast for 10–15 minutes at the top of the oven, until cooked through.

● Around 6–7 minutes before the fish is ready, melt a knob of butter in a sauté pan and sweat the leek for 2 minutes. Add the mussels and toss them in the butter, then pour in the white wine and cover. Cook for around 2 minutes, until all the mussels have opened, then remove the cover and pour in the saffron cream sauce. Boil rapidly for 2 minutes.

● Divide the halibut steaks between 2 prewarmed plates then spoon over the saffron cream sauce, ensuring there are equal amounts of mussels on each plate. Sprinkle with chives and serve with new potatoes or crusty bread.

HIVE HASH

SERVES 2

This dish, to be honest, was a result of trial and error. Everyone knows that crispy potatoes and bacon makes a good breakfast, so we started there. Next, we thought we'd cook them together, so the potatoes would absorb the bacon fat. So far, so good. Then someone pointed out that pancetta's got more flavour than bacon, and we should add chorizo and red onion to give it even more of a boost taste-wise. The result – with a sprinkle of chopped parsley – is a fantastic, one-pan breakfast that provides the perfect start to the day.

INGREDIENTS

Sunflower oil, for frying

15 new potatoes, boiled and chopped in half

4 rashers pancetta, diced into small lardons

1 raw chorizo, thickly sliced

2 eggs

Butter

2 field mushrooms, thickly sliced

1 red onion, sliced

Handful flat-leaf parsley, chopped

Handful watercress, washed

● Heat a drizzle of sunflower oil in a pan and fry the potatoes till they start to crisp; then add the pancetta and chorizo – the oil and fat that seeps out from these will increase the crispiness and flavour of the potatoes.

● While the potatoes are cooking, fry the eggs with a little sunflower oil in a separate pan.

● When the potatoes are crisp and cooked through, add a generous knob of butter, the mushrooms and red onion to the pan, and cook for around 2 minutes.

● Divide the hash between 2 pasta bowls, sprinkle with flat-leaf parsley and arrange a fried egg on top of each.

● Serve immediately with watercress on the side and a mug of tea.

BAKED TURBOT STEAK WITH SAFFRON AÏOLI

SERVES 2

A rare and elusive fish, the turbot is worth seeking out for its incredible, rich flavour and tremendous flexibility – it's just as delicious filleted, in steaks or cooked whole. At The Hive, we buy them from Weymouth skipper Brett Hibbitt, who line-catches the fish in the Race off Portland. He's taken our chefs out on more than one occasion, so they can sample life aboard a sustainable rod-and-line day boat, but so far the trips have failed to yield a single turbot. Perhaps we should leave it to the expert, and concentrate on finding ways to show off this treat of a dish. This simple, baked version is as good as it gets – especially if you make the aïoli a few hours in advance to give the flavours time to intensify.

INGREDIENTS

Light olive oil

4 garlic cloves

10–12 saffron strands

2 eggs

1 lemon, juiced

½ tsp Dijon mustard

2 300–350g turbot steaks

● First, prepare the aïoli. Pour 200ml oil into a small pan then add the garlic and saffron strands, and bring to a gentle simmer. Cook for around 20 minutes, until the garlic cloves have softened and turned a light shade of brown. Remove the garlic and retain, then set the oil aside to cool for at least 30 minutes.

● Place the eggs, lemon juice and mustard into a mixing bowl, and blitz with a hand blender. Very slowly, pour in the cooled oil in a constant stream, mixing continually with the blender. When the mixture reaches the consistency of mayonnaise, add the cooked garlic, sea salt and black pepper. Blend once more, until the garlic is fully puréed. Set aside in the fridge, until the aïoli turns a vibrant saffron-yellow colour.

● Preheat your oven to 220°C/425°F. Place the turbot steaks onto an oiled and seasoned baking tray. Season the fish and drizzle with olive oil, then bake for 10–15 minutes, until cooked through.

● Serve with a generous spoonful of aïoli, new potatoes and a side salad.

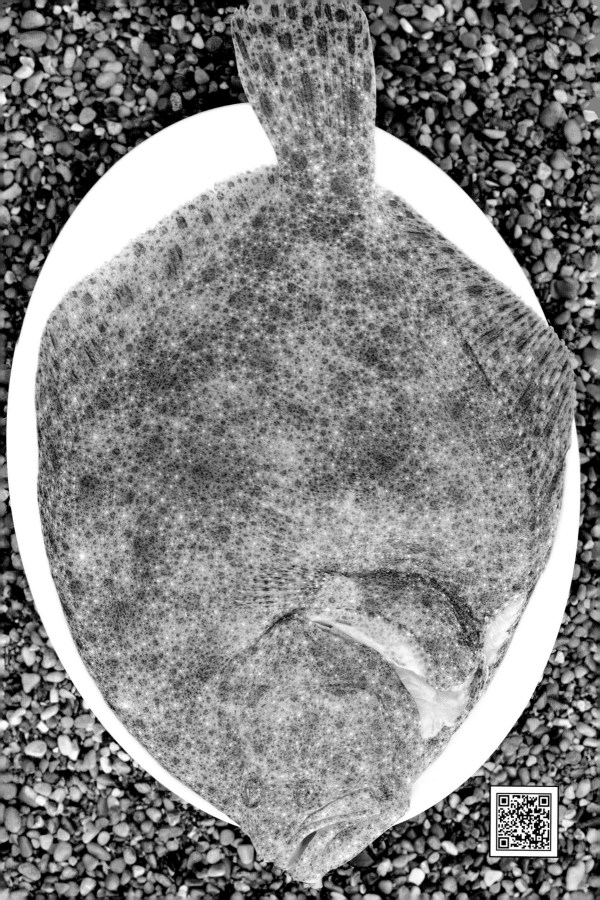

ROASTED HAKE WITH SAUTÉED SPRING GREENS

SERVES 2

The perfect accompaniment to fresh spring greens, hake is an incredibly versatile alternative to cod, with which it shares many characteristics. Its fillets are large and bone-free; and its flesh is soft, white and flaky – and, most importantly, absolutely delicious. One thing the two fish don't have in common, however, is price. Hake, though plentiful off Dorset in spring, is far less in demand, which means it's much, much cheaper. Very popular at The Hive, hake tastes wonderful grilled, poached, pan-fried or – as in this recipe – simply roasted.

INGREDIENTS

½ tsp Dijon mustard

½ tsp wholegrain mustard

50ml white wine vinegar

Light olive oil

Pinch sugar

2 250g hake fillets, scaled and pin-boned

2 baby gem lettuce, cut into quarters

2 handfuls frozen peas

1 red onion, finely diced

Pea shoots, to garnish

1 lemon, cut into wedges

● Preheat your oven to 220°C/425°F. First, make a vinaigrette by spooning the Dijon and wholegrain mustard into a bowl, along with the white wine vinegar, and mixing together. Very slowly, pour in 150ml olive oil in a constant stream, mixing continually. Season to taste with sugar, sea salt and black pepper.

● Place the hake fillets, skin side up, onto an oiled and seasoned roasting tray. Season the fish and drizzle with olive oil, then bake for around 10 minutes, until cooked through.

● Around 2 minutes before the fish is ready, warm a non-stick frying pan. When it's hot, add the lettuce, peas, red onion and a splash of the vinaigrette, and sauté for 1–2 minutes, moving the salad around constantly so that it doesn't burn.

● Arrange the warm salad on 2 plates, add a little more vinaigrette, then place the hake fillets on top. Garnish with pea shoots and lemon wedges, and serve immediately.

GREY MULLET WITH CRAB & JERSEY ROYAL SALAD

SERVES 2

You've got to be careful with grey mullet. The fish caught close to the shore or in estuaries can have a bit of a muddy taste, so you need to ensure you get hold of one that's been lifted from deep water – preferably by a day boat to ensure it's as fresh as possible. Throughout spring, you can often see grey mullet swimming in the River Brit or in the harbour at West Bay. And, to us at The Hive, this signifies it's time to start sourcing some full-flavoured Jersey Royal potatoes and creating this wonderful dish.

INGREDIENTS

10 Jersey Royal potatoes
500g grey mullet fillet, scaled and pin-boned
Olive oil
75g white crab meat

25g butter
Bunch chives, finely chopped
½ lemon, juiced

- Boil the potatoes until soft and set aside in a warm place. Prewarm a non-stick frying pan over a high heat until it's smoking-hot.
- Season the grey mullet fillet and drizzle with olive oil then place, skin side down, in the pan. Do not move for at least 3 minutes. Turn over and repeat on the other side.
- While the fish is cooking, chop the potatoes into small pieces and place in a bowl with the crab meat, butter and a pinch of chives. Gently mix together with the lemon juice, sea salt and freshly ground black pepper.
- Arrange the potato salad in the centre of a warm plate and place the cooked mullet, skin side up, on top. Serve immediately with French beans.

LESLEY WATERS' HOT & SOUR PRAWN SOUP

SERVES 4

This quick and simple soup may be light and refreshing, but – thanks to the chilli and all the Oriental spices included – it still has the ability to warm you up on a cold spring evening. One of our friend Lesley Waters' creations, it marries the plump saltiness of tiger prawns to a broth that positively zings with exotic flavours. Close your eyes and take a mouthful of this, and you can easily imagine the sound of breakers rolling onto Hive Beach are waves lapping the shore of Phang-Nga.

INGREDIENTS

2 tsp cold-pressed sunflower oil
1 red chilli, chopped
2.5cm piece ginger, peeled and
finely chopped
1 garlic clove, crushed
1.2l chicken stock
16 raw tiger prawns, peeled with the
tails left on

1 lime, juiced and zested
2 tbsp Thai Nam Pla fish sauce
150g sugar snap peas, cut in
half lengthways
100g fine rice noodles
Bunch fresh coriander leaves,
roughly chopped

- In a large saucepan or wok, heat the oil. Stir in the chilli, ginger and garlic, and cook for 1 minute. Add the chicken stock and simmer gently for 10 minutes.
- Stir in the tiger prawns, lime juice and zest, Thai Nam Pla fish sauce, sugar snap peas and rice noodles. Bring back to the boil and simmer for a further 2 minutes. Stir in the fresh coriander leaves and serve at once.

SPRING

SEA TROUT WITH CURLY KALE BUBBLE & SQUEAK

SERVES 2

Sea trout is one of those blink-and-you'll-miss-it fish. They come into season in early March and disappear from fishmongers by late June, so you need to make the most of them while they're around. This recipe is a great example of The Hive's 'let the fish flavour speak for itself' philosophy; and we've found sea trout's salmon-like texture and taste work brilliantly with a bubble and squeak made from the wild curly kale we gather from nearby Chesil Bank.

INGREDIENTS

Handful dill, chopped
1 lemon, juiced
Homemade mayonnaise (see page 16)
4–5 medium-sized potatoes, boiled and roughly mashed

100–150g curly kale, trimmed and sliced
Butter
500g sea trout fillet, scaled and pin-boned
Olive oil
2 handfuls plain flour

- Stir the dill and lemon juice into the homemade mayonnaise, and set aside in the fridge.
- Preheat your oven to 220°C/425°F. Boil and roughly mash the potatoes, and set aside.
- Boil the curly kale in salted water for around 5 minutes, until tender. Drain then add to the mashed potatoes along with a small knob of butter, and plenty of sea salt and freshly ground black pepper. Mix and shape into burger-sized bubble-and-squeak cakes.
- Season the sea trout fillet and drizzle with olive oil, then place, skin side down, in a hot frying pan for 2 minutes to crisp up the skin. Remove from the pan and place onto an oiled and seasoned baking tray, then cook in the oven for 6 minutes. Like salmon, sea trout can be served slightly rare if you prefer; the meat turns light-pink when thoroughly cooked.
- While the fish is cooking, arrange the flour on a plate and put the bubble and squeak into it. Cover on all sides and shake off any excess.
- Put a knob of butter and a small drizzle of olive oil into the frying pan you used for the fish, and warm over a medium heat. When hot, fry the bubble-and-squeak cakes for 2–3 minutes on each side, until golden. Try not to move them around as this will cause them to break up.
- Arrange the bubble and squeak on a large plate and top with the sea trout fillet. Serve immediately with the homemade dill-and-lemon mayonnaise.

SMOKED HADDOCK WITH ASPARAGUS BENEDICT

SERVES 2

Asparagus – the fresh-tasting, locally grown variety, anyway – is around for such a short time that it's absolutely vital to make good use of it when it's in season. At The Hive, we get our asparagus from farms across Dorset and the southwest, but you really should try to source yours from as close by as possible – the less food miles involved, the better. This lovely combination of salty smoked haddock, creamy Hollandaise and juicy asparagus may be considered by many to be a breakfast dish. But when something is this delicious, why limit yourself to only serving it before 11am?

INGREDIENTS

8–10 asparagus spears
350–400g smoked haddock
600ml milk
1 bay leaf

2 English muffins, sliced in half
2 eggs
Homemade Hollandaise sauce (see page 16)
Handful chives, chopped

- Place a pan of water on a high heat and bring to the boil.
- Snap off the woody bases of the asparagus spears, then cook in the boiling water for 2–3 minutes. Remove and set aside in a warm place. Let the water continue to simmer gently.
- Place the haddock into a pan with the milk and bay leaf, and gently bring up to the boil. Around 1 minute after the liquid reaches boiling point, remove the fish with a slotted spoon and set aside in a warm place. Discard the liquid.
- Put the English muffins on to toast.
- Add a splash of vinegar to the simmering water and carefully crack in the eggs. Poach for 2–3 minutes.
- Put the toasted muffins onto a pre-warmed plate, place the smoked haddock on top and arrange the asparagus spears by the side. Place the poached egg on the haddock and spoon over some of the Hollandaise sauce. Garnish with chives and serve.

SCALLOP SCAMPI WITH HOMEMADE TARTARE SAUCE

SERVES 2

There's a reason why scampi has held its own on UK pub menus for the best part of three decades. It has always been created with the most readily available seafood, which in years gone by would have been langoustines. Soaring demand for this succulent shellfish has seen the end of that, though, and modern pub scampi tends to be made from a processed fish paste. Our posh scampi – which flies out of The Hive's kitchen in spring – is made from scallops, which provide the same soft, sweet white meat as langoustines. One taste and you'll see exactly why this deep-fried dish became so incredibly popular.

INGREDIENTS

Sunflower oil, for deep-frying

14 scallops

2 handfuls plain flour

1 egg

100ml milk

2 large handfuls white breadcrumbs

Homemade tartare sauce (see page 17)

1 lemon, cut into wedges

- Preheat the sunflower oil to 180°C/350°F in a large pan or deep-fat fryer.
- Roll the scallops in the flour until they are totally covered. Shake off any excess.
- Whisk the egg and milk together in a bowl, then dip each of the scallops into the mixture. Roll the scallops in the breadcrumbs and place on a separate plate ready for frying.
- Deep-fry the coated scallops for 3–4 minutes, until crisp and golden-brown. Remove and place on a piece of kitchen paper to soak up any excess oil. Season generously with sea salt.
- Divide the scallops between 2 plates and add a generous dollop of homemade tartare sauce to the side. Garnish with lemon wedges, and serve immediately with chips and salad.

SMOKED MACKEREL WITH HORSERADISH CRÈME FRAÎCHE

SERVES 2

This wonderful, quick-to-make spring salad may be zinging with all the fresh colours of the season, but the peppered smoked mackerel at its heart would have been – believe it or not – caught in frostier winter months. When we turn up our central heating, mackerel head for deeper water to build up the fat reserves that make the final, smoked product so tasty. The seasonality of the fish – which can simply be taken from the freezer and defrosted in less than an hour – doesn't matter in this case; that of the herbs, leaves and vegetables accompanying it most certainly does.

INGREDIENTS

8 new potatoes
2 tbsp creamed horseradish
2 cooked beetroot, chopped into small pieces

Small tub crème fraîche
Small bunch chives, chopped
2 peppered smoked mackerel fillets
2 bunches watercress

● Boil the new potatoes until they're cooked. They are ready when you insert a thin knife into them and they slip off easily.
● Mix together the creamed horseradish, beetroot, crème fraîche and chives in a bowl with sea salt and freshly ground pepper. Slice the cooked new potatoes in half and add to the crème fraîche mixture.
● Flake the peppered smoked mackerel fillets into another bowl.
● Divide the watercress into 2 salad bowls, add the horseradish crème fraîche and potato mixture, and top with the flaked smoked mackerel.

JOHN DORY IN A COCKLE, BABY LEEK & CIDER BROTH

SERVES 2

This classic Dorset broth is absolutely bursting with local seasonal flavours. John Dory makes a good base for the soup as it can more than handle the salty cockles, peppery leeks and strong farmhouse cider that we use when making this dish at The Hive, though we've found that turbot makes a good substitute. As spring-like as brief showers and cool evenings, this very simple recipe is ideal for warming you up after a day spent outside.

INGREDIENTS

2 400–500g John Dory, filleted and pin-boned
1 onion, diced
8–10 baby leeks, trimmed
Splash cider

10–15 cockles
200ml fish stock (see page 15)
Handful fresh parsley, chopped
1 lemon, cut into wedges

● Preheat a hot grill. Place the John Dory fillets onto an oiled and seasoned baking tray, skin side up, then season and drizzle with olive oil.

● Prewarm a sauté pan until it's hot. Add the onion, baby leeks and cider, then cover and simmer for around 3 minutes.

● Grill the John Dory fillets for 6–7 minutes, until cooked through.

● While the fish is cooking, add the cockles and fish stock to the broth and boil vigorously for 3–4 minutes, until the liquid is reduced by half. Season with plenty of sea salt and freshly ground black pepper.

● Place the John Dory fillets on a piece of kitchen paper to absorb as much excess oil as possible, then divide them between 2 prewarmed bowls. Spoon over the broth, ensuring there are an equal number of cockles and leeks in each dish.

● Finish with a sprinkling of parsley and serve immediately with lemon wedges on the side.

SARDINES ON TOAST NEAPOLITAN

SERVES 2

Though this classic dish originated in the ports of southern Italy, we think our West Dorset version holds its own – mainly because the sardines we use, plucked straight from the sea in front of The Hive, are so ridiculously fresh. This recipe – more familiar to the older generation than youthful fish-lovers – works well as a snack or a main meal, and is very simple to prepare. And there's plenty of scope for making the tomato sauce your own by altering the amounts of wine and balsamic vinegar. We've found that a certain level of acidity cuts through the oiliness of the sardines quite wonderfully.

INGREDIENTS

Olive oil

1 red onion, diced

2 garlic cloves, finely chopped

440g good-quality tinned tomatoes

Glass red wine

25ml balsamic vinegar

Bunch flat-leaf parsley, chopped

100g black olives, pitted

6–8 whole sardines, depending on size

2 thick slices granary bread

1 lemon, cut into wedges

● Preheat a hot grill. Put a splash of olive oil into a sauté pan then sweat the red onion and garlic for 2–3 minutes, until soft. Pour in the tomatoes and red wine, and simmer for around 10 minutes. Add the balsamic vinegar, flat-leaf parsley and olives, and simmer for 5 minutes more. Set aside in a warm place.

● While the sauce is cooking, place the sardines onto an oiled and seasoned baking tray. Season the fish and drizzle with olive oil, then grill for 6–8 minutes, until cooked through.

● Toast the granary bread and divide between 2 plates. Pour the sauce over the toasted bread and place the grilled sardines on top. Finish with a sprinkling of flat-leaf parsley and a lemon wedge, and serve while hot.

SPICED SPIDER CRAB GRATIN

SERVES 2

This is one of those dishes we serve at The Hive that involves absolutely no food miles. Hive Beach seems to be something of a romantic destination for spider crabs, who arrive in their hundreds at the end of spring to breed just behind the sand shelf a few metres out to sea. Were you to snorkel anywhere between West Bay and Cogden Beach at this time of year, you'd witness the alien-like spectacle of these enormous crabs crawling over each other in an effort to get their rocks off. If you're brave enough, you could even grab one to create this fabulous recipe with.

INGREDIENTS

2 spider crabs, meat removed
Handful spring onions, sliced
Handful chives, finely chopped
½ tsp mustard
2 lemons, juiced

Pinch cayenne pepper
Small piece parmesan, grated
2 handfuls breadcrumbs
Clarified butter

● Preheat a hot grill. Take the meat (including that from the legs and claws) from your spider crabs and put into a mixing bowl. Retain and clean the shell to serve the gratin in.
● Check the crab meat carefully for bits of shell, then combine with the spring onions, chives, mustard, lemon juice and cayenne pepper (feel free to add more if you like your food spicy). Season with sea salt and black pepper, and spoon the mixture into the empty crab shell.
● Grate some parmesan into the breadcrumbs and add a little clarified butter. Mix together and arrange on top of the crab-meat mixture.
● Grill for a few minutes, until hot throughout and golden-brown on top, then serve.

SUMMER

BAKED JOHN DORY WITH ROSEMARY & CHERRY TOMATOES

SERVES 2

It might not be much of a looker, but what the John Dory lacks in beauty it makes up for in taste. And, as they're fairly plentiful off the Dorset coast throughout the summer, we've developed several ways of serving them up at The Hive. This delicious baked version is one of our favourites – combining, as it does, the buttery taste of its delicate flesh with the sharpness of the hot cherry tomatoes. We'd even go as far as to say it's perfect with a cold bottle of crisp white wine.

INGREDIENTS

2 whole 500–600g John Dory, gutted

Olive oil

2 sprigs rosemary

1 punnet cherry tomatoes

- Preheat your oven to 180°C/350°F. Place the whole John Dorys onto a roasting tray, then drizzle with olive oil, sprinkle generously with sea salt, and stuff as much rosemary and cherry tomatoes as you'd like into the belly.
- Bake for 10–15 minutes, until cooked through.
- Serve immediately, while the tomatoes are still piping-hot inside.
- At The Hive, we like to send out this dish with a side salad, buttered new potatoes and a glass of dry white wine.

THE HIVE COLD SHELLFISH PLATTER

SERVES 2

Our signature summer dish is something of an inexact science. We make this colossal crustacean creation by handpicking the freshest shellfish we have to hand and piling it up in ever-more artistic arrangements before serving. For the sake of this recipe, we've selected our favourite combination. It's worth remembering that fresh shellfish is loaded with essential minerals, protein, vitamins B12 and C, and Omega 3 fatty acids that help keep your cholesterol levels low. It also tastes absolutely amazing.

INGREDIENTS

1 whole lobster

1 whole crab

4 oysters

Seaweed

6 langoustines

6 crevette prawns

1 lemon, cut into wedges

● Prepare the lobster, crab and oysters according to the instructions on pages 13 and 14 or, alternatively, ask your fishmonger to do it for you.

● We like to use seaweed as the base for our shellfish platter as it gives everything a wonderful splash of marine colour. Make sure you blanch it in boiling salted water for a few minutes first. Then, once boiled, place it in cold water to refresh it and bring out the vibrant green hue.

● Have fun arranging the lobster, crab, oysters, langoustines and crevette prawns on top of the seaweed. When you're happy with your creation, serve with crusty bread and wedges of lemon. Don't forget the finger bowls.

PLAICE GOUJONS WITH MINTED MUSHY PEAS

SERVES 2

We all know that kids love goujons – but so, it seems, do plenty of adults. This dish is a huge summer hit at The Hive and it's certainly not just the under-10s who order it. The delicate, moist flesh of plaice goes wonderfully with the light crispiness of the coating, and we've found that a bowl of freshly made minted peas – our take on the chip-shop mushy variety – is the ideal accompaniment. Serve the goujons on a big sharing platter with a portion of straight-from-the-fryer chips and let everyone dig in and help themselves…

INGREDIENTS

Sunflower oil, for deep-frying

2 cups garden peas

50g butter

Good splash double cream

Handful mint, roughly chopped

2 450g plaice fillets, skinned

50g plain flour

2 eggs, lightly beaten

2 large handfuls white breadcrumbs

- Preheat the sunflower oil to 180°C/350°F in a large pan or deep-fat fryer.
- Bring a pan of water up to the boil. Add the garden peas and cook until tender, then drain and place into a bowl with the butter, cream, mint and a pinch of sea salt. Blitz until mushy with a hand blender. Set aside in a warm place.
- Cut the plaice fillets into finger-width strips. Season the flour with sea salt and spread it out on a large plate. Place the beaten eggs in a shallow bowl next to this, and lay out the breadcrumbs on a plate alongside the eggs.
- Take each piece of plaice and coat it with the flour. Then dip it into the eggs and roll in the breadcrumbs till thoroughly covered.
- Carefully add the strips of plaice, a few at a time, to the hot oil. Fry for 2–3 minutes, until golden-brown. Remove and place on a piece of kitchen paper to absorb excess oil, then keep hot on a pre-warmed dish. Reheat the oil before putting in each fresh batch.
- When all goujons are cooked, serve with the minted mushy peas and a handful of chips.

ROASTED GURNARD WITH OLIVE OIL & SEA SALT

SERVES 2

Gurnard – also known as sea robin due to its wing-like fins, may be a little on the unusual-looking side. But this shouldn't put you off. It's cheap and plentiful for a start, and its firm texture makes it a more than viable alternative to cod or haddock. Here at The Hive, we like to bring the fish's stunning flavour to the fore, and we believe it's best served without the distractions of spice, sauce or marinade. This roasted version, dressed only with olive oil and sea salt, is absolutely delicious. If you must have an accompaniment, then a simple salad and a cold bottle of wine are perfect.

INGREDIENTS

2 whole 500–600g gurnard,
gutted and scaled

Olive oil

- Preheat your oven to 180°C/350°F. Place your gurnards onto a roasting tray, then drizzle with olive oil and sprinkle generously with sea salt.
- Roast for 10–15 minutes, until cooked through.
- Serve immediately before the fish have a chance to cool.

LEMON SOLE WITH ANCHOVY & HERB BUTTER

SERVES 2

The lemon sole – a flatfish that inhabits the stony areas of the seabed, around 200 metres down – is a must-have dish at The Hive when it's in season. The meat content is high and the flesh has a delicate, sweet taste that goes wonderfully with the saltiness of the anchovies in this recipe. It's best served with new potatoes, which you can use to soak up all that extra butter, and – naturally – a cold glass of white wine.

INGREDIENTS

2 500–600g lemon sole, gutted and skinned
Olive oil
12 anchovies
150g butter

1 bunch parsley, roughly chopped
1 bunch dill, roughly chopped
1 bunch chives, roughly chopped
1 lemon, zested and juiced

● Preheat your oven to 180°C/350°F.
● Place the lemon sole onto a roasting tray, then drizzle with olive oil, sprinkle with sea salt and roast for 10–15 minutes, until cooked through.
● While the fish is cooking, prepare the anchovy and herb butter. Roughly chop 8 of the anchovies and add them to the butter, along with the parsley, dill and chives. Throw in the lemon zest and half the lemon juice, and mix well until all the ingredients are combined.
● Remove the lemon sole from the oven and place a generous portion of anchovy and herb butter on top of each one.
● Put the fish back into the oven for 1 minute or until all the butter has melted, then garnish with the remaining anchovies and serve.

MACKEREL WITH RED ONION & RED PEPPER SALSA

SERVES 2

This dish reappears on The Hive menu every summer, and it's as much of a favourite with us as it is with our customers. Almost all the mackerel we use are line-caught by our suppliers' day boats in West Bay – forget food miles, we're thinking in feet here – and at certain times of the year, the sea off Hive Beach seems to be almost bubbling with shoals of this delicious, oily fish. The sharp combination of red onion and pepper in this recipe works wonders with the dense flavour of the mackerel, which is best served straight from the grill.

INGREDIENTS

4 mackerel, divided into 8 fillets
Olive oil
1 red onion, finely diced

1 red pepper, finely diced
1 lemon
1 bunch chives, finely chopped

● Preheat your grill. Season the mackerel fillets with sea salt and drizzle with olive oil.

● Put the mackerel fillets onto a tray, skin side up, and place under a hot grill for 4–6 minutes, until cooked through.

● To make the salsa, add the diced red onion and red pepper to a bowl, then drizzle generously with olive oil and a squeeze of lemon. Throw in the chives and season with sea salt before mixing it all together.

● As soon as the mackerel fillets are cooked, slide them onto a pre-warmed plate and spoon salsa over the top. Serve immediately with lemon wedges and a hunk of bread.

MUSSELS WITH WHITE WINE, HERBS, GARLIC & CREAM

SERVES 2

The mussels we use at The Hive hail from the point at which the River Fowey spills into Lyme Bay. This isn't just blind local loyalty. The mussels from here are rope-grown (ie, cultivated on lines that float in the warm, nutrient-rich water close to the river surface), and we believe this makes them meatier and ultimately much more tasty. Our no-frills take on classic moules marinière is best enjoyed with bottle of chilled wine and a hunk of crusty bread to mop up the sauce. It simply flies out of The Hive kitchen in summertime.

INGREDIENTS

900g mussels
1 shallot, diced
2 garlic cloves, finely chopped
20g butter
2 bay leaves

1 sprig thyme
100ml white wine
100ml double cream
1 bunch parsley, finely chopped

- Wash the mussels and discard any that do not close when tapped.
- Put the shallot and garlic into a large lidded saucepan along with the butter, and cook for a few minutes until they start to soften.
- Add in the bay leaves and thyme, then pour in the mussels and white wine. Place the lid on the pan to steam open the mussels.
- Cook for around 3 minutes, shaking the sealed pan occasionally, until the mussels have opened. Pour in the cream and cook for another minute.
- Divide the mussels between 2 large dishes, pour over the sauce from the pan and sprinkle with the chopped parsley. Serve immediately.

WEYMOUTH CRAB & AVOCADO SALAD

SERVES 2

We're very fond of a Weymouth crab here at The Hive. Those that are landed in the buzzing harbour town – a few miles along the Jurassic Coast from Burton Bradstock – tend to provide deliciously creamy and sweet white meat, which is the ideal accompaniment to the range of summer salads on our menu. The avocado and herbs in this dish combine perfectly with the crab to create the ultimate light lunch; and we get a lot of orders for this along with a cold bottle of white wine when the sun is shining.

INGREDIENTS

1 cooked crab (to provide 150g white meat)
2 medium avocados, peeled, stoned and finely cubed
2 plum tomatoes, roughly chopped
1 red pepper, finely chopped
4 spring onions, roughly chopped

Bunch flat-leaf parsley, roughly chopped
4 sprigs dill
Small bunch chives, roughly chopped
Handful crunchy salad leaves
Olive oil
1 lemon

● Separate off the white meat from the crab. Check it carefully to make sure it doesn't contain any fragments of shell, then set aside.

● Next, create the salad by tossing the avocados, tomatoes, red pepper, spring onions, parsley, dill and chives together with the salad leaves. Drizzle it generously with olive oil and a good squeeze of lemon, and season with sea salt and black pepper.

● Add the white crab meat to the salad and toss carefully so that it coats all the leaves. Serve in a large bowl for everyone to share.

HAKE WITH CHILLI & TOMATO CHUTNEY

SERVES 2

Hake comes from the same family as cod and haddock, and is a popular dish at The Hive due to its light and flaky texture, which goes well with more highly flavoured accompaniments. It is particularly delicious when teamed with the 'sea-taste' of rock samphire – which also goes under the alias of sea asparagus – and the light spiciness of a chilli and tomato chutney. Go easy with the additional seasoning in this recipe. The samphire packs a seriously salty punch.

INGREDIENTS

1kg tomatoes, chopped

500g red onions, finely sliced

4 garlic cloves, sliced

1 red chilli, chopped

4cm piece ginger, peeled and chopped

250g brown sugar

150ml red wine vinegar

5 cardamom seeds

½ tsp paprika

2 large hake fillets, scaled and pin-boned

Olive oil

200g samphire

● First, make the chilli and tomato chutney. Tip the tomatoes, red onions, garlic, chilli, ginger, sugar, red wine vinegar, cardamom seeds and paprika into a large, heavy-based pan and bring to a gentle simmer, stirring frequently.

● Simmer the mixture for 1 hour, then gently bring it up to a boil so that it turns dark, jammy and shiny. Once made, the chutney will keep for up to six weeks.

● Arrange the hake fillets on a baking tray, skin side up, and season with olive oil and sea salt. Place under a hot grill for 5–6 minutes, until cooked through.

● Once the hake fillets are ready, remove them from the grill and set aside. Place the samphire into a hot, non-stick frying pan and drizzle with a little olive oil. Sauté for around 1 minute.

● When the samphire is cooked, arrange it on 2 plates and place the hake fillets on top. Spoon a generous portion of warmed chilli and tomato chutney over the fish and serve immediately.

CHARGRILLED BLACK BREAM WITH LEMON & ROSEMARY

SERVES 2

When black bream is fresh out of the water – as it always is when it comes into The Hive – it's one of those fish to which the old adage 'less is more' applies. We certainly do as little to it as possible before serving. That's not because we're lazy; we just believe the flavour speaks for itself. This simple, chargrilled cooking method – in which the firm flesh is perfectly complemented by tart lemon and aromatic rosemary – brings out the best in it. Try it with a crisp, green salad and a portion of chunky chips, and wash it all down with an ice-cold cider.

INGREDIENTS

1 lemon
Whole 500–600g black bream, gutted
and scaled

2 sprigs rosemary
Olive oil

- Preheat your oven to 180°C/350°F.
- First, slice the lemon into quarters and stuff it into the belly of the black bream along with the rosemary sprigs. Sprinkle the fish generously with sea salt.
- Place onto a hot chargrill or barbecue for 4 minutes, then turn and leave to cook for another 4 minutes.
- Place the black bream onto a lightly oiled baking tray and put it into the oven. Bake for 4 minutes, until cooked through. Serve while still piping-hot.

DOVER SOLE
IN PARSLEY
& GARLIC BUTTER

SERVES 2

The Dover sole is the Rolls-Royce of the fish world. It is the tastiest member of the sole family and, with its firm, deliciously delicate flesh, is often best served simply. This recipe, which goes well with a few new potatoes to soak up the butter and a glass of something crisp and fizzy to cut through the garlicky sauce, is one of the finest we've developed at The Hive. If summer could ever be summed up in a meal, this is it.

INGREDIENTS

2 500–600g Dover sole, gutted
and skinned
Olive oil
1 bunch parsley, roughly chopped

2 garlic cloves, chopped
1 lemon, zested and juiced
150g butter

● Preheat your oven to 180°C/350°F. Place the 2 sole onto a roasting tray, skin side down, then drizzle with olive oil and sprinkle with sea salt. Roast for 10–15 minutes, until cooked through.

● While the fish is cooking, add the parsley, garlic, lemon zest and half the lemon juice to the butter, and throw in a pinch of sea salt. Mix all the ingredients together.

● When the fish is cooked, place a generous portion of the parsley and garlic butter on top of each and return to the oven for around a minute.

● Serve as soon as the butter has melted.

Kingfisher Brixham
Direct Seafoods

TEMPURA COD WITH MINTED MUSHY PEAS

SERVES 2

Our version of fish and chips – the British seaside classic – is by far and away the bestselling item on The Hive's menu. Fresh, firm cod, wrapped in the lightest of tempura batters and accompanied by crisp, hot chips and our minty take on mushy peas, tastes wonderful at all times of the year. But eating it al fresco at The Hive on a hot summer's day – with the sun warming the back of your neck and waves rattling pebbles just a few feet away – seems to make it even more delicious. Kids, we've found, love it with a can of Coke; adults with a glass of wine. Nans and granddads? With a cup of tea, of course.

INGREDIENTS

Sunflower oil, for deep-frying

3 cups plain flour

150ml sparkling water

Handful flat-leaf parsley, roughly chopped

2 250g cod fillets, scaled and pin-boned

2 cups garden peas

50g butter

Good splash double cream

Handful mint, roughly chopped

● Preheat the sunflower oil to 180°C/350°F in a large pan or deep-fat fryer. You need to put in enough oil to fully cover the fish.

● Whisk together 2 cups of flour with the sparkling water to create a thin batter. Mix in the chopped flat-leaf parsley and set aside.

● Spread out the remaining flour and plenty of sea salt on a baking tray, and coat the cod fillets thoroughly with the mixture. Dip the fish fillets into the batter, ensuring they are fully covered; and deep-fry, skin side down, for 4–6 minutes (depending on thickness), until the batter is golden and the fish is cooked through. Remove and place on a piece of kitchen paper to absorb excess oil.

● Bring a pan of water up to the boil. Add the garden peas and cook until tender, then drain and place into a bowl with the butter, cream, mint and a pinch of sea salt. Blitz until mushy with a hand blender.

● Divide the tempura cod fillets between 2 prewarmed plates and arrange the minted mushy peas alongside – either on the plate or in a separate ramekin. Serve with hot chips, and plenty of sea salt and vinegar.

GRILLED LOBSTER WITH GARLIC BUTTER

SERVES 2

When lobster is served this simply, only the very best will do. All of the lobsters we use at The Hive are caught off Burton Bradstock, Freshwater and Weymouth, and are delivered to us each morning, which absolutely guarantees their freshness. Unsurprisingly, this dish – which complements the succulent meat with a delicious, herby, garlicky sauce – is in hot demand with our customers during the summer months.

INGREDIENTS

2 garlic cloves, finely chopped
1 bunch parsley, roughly chopped
1 lemon, zested and juiced

100g butter
1 whole cooked lobster

● To make the sauce, add the garlic, parsley and lemon zest to the butter. Throw in some sea salt and half the lemon juice, and mix well.
● Preheat your grill. Cut the cooked lobster in half and spoon the garlic butter onto the exposed white meat. Place under a medium grill for a few minutes, until the butter has melted and the lobster meat has been warmed through.
● Serve immediately with salad and a bowl of chips.

SEABASS FOR TWO

SERVES 2

Though we regularly offer larger seabass – some of which will feed up to 10 people – this meal for two is justifiably one of the most popular on the Hive's menu. Our bass are line-caught by local skipper Brett Hibbitt in the Race off Portland Bill, where three tides meet and cause the water to 'boil', and are brought to us within two hours of being lifted from the sea. As sea-to-plate dishes go, it can't be beaten. Especially when eaten outdoors with a glass of cold rosé and the sun on your back.

INGREDIENTS

Olive oil

1kg fresh, line-caught wild seabass, scaled and gutted

2 sprigs rosemary

1 lemon, cut into 4 wedges

- Preheat your oven to 200°C/400°F.
- Pour a splash of olive oil onto a baking tray and place the seabass onto it. Rub some oil over the fish's body with your hands and sprinkle sea salt onto both sides.
- Stuff the rosemary and lemon wedges into the belly.
- Put the seabass into the oven for 15–20 minutes, until the skin is golden-brown and the flesh has cooked through.
- Serve with new potatoes or chips, and a bowl of fresh salad.

OUR SUPPLIERS: STEVE ELSWORTH, BURTON BRADSTOCK

'I was born and bred in Burton Bradstock,' says fisherman Steve Elsworth (*left*). 'From an early age I was fishing down on Hive beach and when I got a bit older I started going out mackerelling with some of the old locals. I worked on a trawler for a while, then, around six years ago, I had the opportunity to buy my own boat. I've been running it ever since.

'I park at The Hive and work from the shore outwards to about four miles to the west, as far as Golden Cap. The majority of my fishing is crab and lobster, and I put out strings of five pots, which are left out there all the time. I fish them as and when the weather lets me. In the summer, I start going to sea at five in the morning. Mid-morning, I ring The Hive to see what they require and then I take it straight down there – live – which the holidaymakers love seeing, I can tell you.

'When you're doing this job you get to know what's a good crab and what's not going to be quite such good crab just by looking. You can tell by the weight and by the colour of the shell – when they've just changed their casing, they're a lot better-tasting. The Hive always gets the best of what I've got. Tim Attrill, one of the chefs there, had the biggest crab I've ever landed, which was just short of 10 pounds. It was huge; bigger than my kids when they were born. They sold that as a meal for two, I think.

'I'm down at The Hive most days – if I'm not landing fish, I normally pop in for a cup of coffee. I started working for the Attrills at the age of 18 when they had the pub in the village, and I've known Steve [owner of The Hive] for too many years. He takes around 95 per cent of my lobster, as he likes to work with sustainable, fresh, local produce. It's a very Burton Bradstock connection.'

Steve Elsworth (07801 994181). Alternatively, ask for Steve at The Hive.

SEARED SCALLOPS WITH PANCETTA & CHORIZO

SERVES 2

One of our bestselling summertime dishes, this combination of delicate, fresh-from-the-water Lyme Bay scallops with salty pancetta and spicy chorizo goes out of the kitchen as fast as we can make it. We recently prepared this recipe on our stall at the Weymouth Seafood Festival – mainly to show just how easy it was to make – and ended up selling nearly 100 kilos in platefuls to hungry onlookers. It may be ridiculously simple, but it's one of the tastiest dishes you'll ever make.

INGREDIENTS

6 scallops
Olive oil
100g pancetta, cut into lardons
100g chorizo, cut into slices the size of
a five-pence piece

50g butter
1 bunch parsley, roughly chopped
1 lemon
Salad leaves

● Place a heavy-bottomed frying pan onto a high heat. Season the scallops with sea salt and olive oil, and add them to the pan once it's hot.

● Turn each scallop after 45–60 seconds (depending on their size) and add the pancetta and chorizo to the pan. Make sure the scallops are golden-brown where they've been in contact with the pan.

● Add the butter, parsley and a squeeze of lemon after another 45–60 seconds, then remove from the heat and leave to stand for 1 minute.

● Serve on a bed of salad leaves, with a hunk of granary bread on the side.

BAKED DABS WITH LEMON & GARLIC BUTTER

SERVES 2

The common dab is a flatfish, which lives on the sandy sea-bottom as far down as 100 metres. Plentiful in Lyme Bay during the summer months, this inexpensive dish is incredibly popular with our customers at The Hive due to its light taste and soft, sweet texture. We believe the flavour speaks for itself, so we tend to serve it fairly unadulterated – such as in this wonderfully tasty yet incredibly straightforward recipe – though we've found that a bottle of Palmers Bridport ale makes a very pleasant accompaniment.

INGREDIENTS

4 whole 300-400g dabs, gutted
Olive oil
2 garlic cloves, crushed

Butter
1 lemon, juiced

● Preheat your oven to 180°C/350°F. Place the dabs onto a roasting tray, score the flesh, then drizzle on the olive oil and sprinkle generously with sea salt.

● Place the garlic, butter and lemon juice in a food processor, and blitz together to create a garlic butter.

● Bake the dabs for 10–15 minutes, until cooked through. Remove from the oven, spread garlic butter on top and bake for around 2 minutes, until the butter has melted.

● Serve immediately with a light salad and a few new potatoes. And don't forget the beer.

SMOKED SALMON & SCRAMBLED EGGS

SERVES 2

One of the most popular choices on our Breakfast Club menu, this simple combination of salty salmon and creamy, local eggs has been dished up at The Hive since we first started back in 1991. We've found it's essential to use good-quality smoked salmon and free-range eggs in this dish, and the more freshly baked the granary bread, the better. Try it with a glass of Bucks Fizz or Champagne for a truly luxurious breakfast.

INGREDIENTS

6 eggs
Splash cream
4 slices smoked salmon

Handful chives, chopped
2 slices granary bread, toasted
Butter

- Preheat a frying pan and, while it's warming up, whisk the eggs with the cream. Season to taste (don't go overboard, though, as the salmon is likely to be very salty).
- Finely slice the smoked salmon and chop the chives. Then, just before you start cooking the eggs, put the slices of bread on to toast.
- Place a generous knob of butter in the frying pan and, as it starts to melt, add in the egg mixture and stir until creamy. Continue cooking until the eggs reach the desired texture.
- Roll the egg mixture in the smoked salmon and chives, and serve on the hot toast.

SEABASS NIÇOISE

SERVES 2

Though the Blue-fin Tuna Regeneration Programme – of which we're a big supporter – is working wonders at replenishing stocks of that endangered fish, it does mean the once-ubiquitous Niçoise salad has become something of a distant memory. We believe it's too good a dish to consign to the culinary dustbin, though, and have found it can be wonderfully recreated with several species of fish – most notably the seabass. Its firm texture and mild flavour complements the freshness of the salad and vegetables, and goes very well with hard-boiled eggs. All in all, it's a perfect dish for a lazy summer evening.

INGREDIENTS

2 400g seabass fillets, scaled and pin-boned
Olive oil
Handful French beans
8 new potatoes
8 anchovies

Handful olives, each one cut in half
Bunch parsley, roughly chopped
2 eggs, hard-boiled and cut into quarters

● Prewarm a frying pan over a medium heat. Drizzle the seabass fillets with olive oil, and season with sea salt and freshly ground black pepper.

● Place the seabass fillets in the pan, skin side down, and cook for 3–4 minutes, until the skin turns golden-brown. Turn the fillets over, remove from the heat and leave for 3 minutes. The residual heat from the pan will cook them through.

● Bring a saucepan of water up to the boil and add the French beans. Blanch for 2–3 minutes, then remove and place in cold water to cool and stop them from cooking further. Drain and set aside.

● Boil the new potatoes in the same pan. They are ready when you insert a thin knife into them and they slip off easily. Once they're cooked, cut each in half.

● Place the new potatoes, blanched French beans, anchovies, olives and parsley into a bowl and mix well. Drizzle with olive oil and season with sea salt.

● Arrange generous spoonfuls of the Niçoise salad mixture on 2 plates and place the seabass fillets on top. Decorate with the hard-boiled egg quarters and serve.

SQUID WITH A CHILLI, CORIANDER & LIME BUTTER

SERVES 2

You know that summer's arrived when you see this light dish make its first appearance on The Hive menu. Squid is plentiful in Lyme Bay at this time of year, and there's something about its unique texture and flavour that seems to remind people of Mediterranean holidays – especially if they're eating it beside the beach at Burton Bradstock with the warm sun on their necks. This spicy and zingy sauce brings out the best in the squid. Make sure you've got a bottle of ice-cold beer to hand and a hunk of bread to mop up all the juices.

INGREDIENTS

1 red chilli, finely diced
Bunch coriander, roughly chopped
1 lime, zested and juiced

150g butter
2 tbsp olive oil
500g squid, cut into ½ cm rings

● First, prepare the sauce. Add the chopped chilli, coriander and lime zest to the butter, then pour in the lime juice. Season with sea salt and mix together.
● Pour the olive oil into a frying pan and place onto a high heat. Once it's hot, throw in the squid rings. Turn after 50 seconds or so and add a tablespoon of the chilli, coriander and lime butter.
● The dish will be ready once the butter has melted and the squid rings have turned white. Serve immediately with a hunk of bread.

BURTON BRADSTOCK BROWN CRAB SALAD

SERVES 1

One of our most iconic dishes, this take on the classic crab salad is one we all look forward to chalking up on the menu. Brown crabs spend the cold winter months in a bit of a sloth-like state, and this inactivity means the meat gets watery and unappetising. Once the sea warms up a little, though, they head to shallower water and move around a lot more – improving the texture and volume of the meat dramatically. If you're feeling brave enough, you could open your crab in the traditional Hive way – by smashing its shell with a stone from the beach…

INGREDIENTS

1 live brown crab
Handful chives, chopped

1 lemon, cut into 4 segments
Homemade mayonnaise (see page 16)

- This dish really does require a crab that's as fresh as possible, so it's worth preparing one according to the instructions on page 13. Alternatively, you can ask your fishmonger to do it for you.
- Stir the chives and juice of 2 lemon segments into the homemade mayonnaise.
- Serve the crab whole with a generous dollop of mayonnaise, the 2 remaining lemon segments and a portion of crusty bread.

SKATE WING WITH BROWN BUTTER & CAPER SAUCE

SERVES 2

One of several members of the ray family found all year round in Lyme Bay, skate is known for its firm, meaty flesh, which slides easily from the bones in its wings. It's certainly very desirable at The Hive, where we serve it with simple salads, bowls of buttery new potatoes and glasses of ice-cold beer, and it seems to suit warm summer evenings very well indeed. This traditional recipe complements its fine, delicate flavour with a no-frills sauce of creamy brown butter and tangy capers.

INGREDIENTS

1 cup plain flour
2 400–500g skate wings, skinned
Olive oil
150g butter

½ lemon, juiced
2 tbsp capers
Bunch flat-leaf parsley, roughly chopped

● Warm a frying pan over a medium heat. Spread the plain flour out on a plate and coat the skate wings on both sides.

● Drizzle olive oil into the frying pan and add in the skate wings, thick side up. Cook for 3–4 minutes, until golden-brown on the bottom, then turn and cook for another 3–4 minutes. Remove from the heat and rest for 2 minutes.

● Check to see whether the skate wings have cooked through (see page 11). If not, return to the pan for another minute or so.

● Place a saucepan onto a high heat and, when hot, add the butter. Once the butter has melted and started to turn golden-brown, add the lemon juice, capers and flat-leaf parsley, and remove from the heat.

● Arrange the skate wings on 2 prewarmed plates and drizzle with the brown butter and caper sauce. Serve immediately.

HUSS FISHFINGERS WITH HOMEMADE TARTARE SAUCE

SERVES 2

Our twist on this classic children's comfort dish has proved to be as much of a favourite with adults as it is with kids. Though huss may be familiar to the older generation – who will know it by its more old-fashioned name of rock salmon – the popularity of this tasty fish has waned dramatically over the past few decades. It comes, though, from a very sustainable source and provides a great alternative to cod. And it goes brilliantly with the tanginess of the tartare sauce in this recipe.

INGREDIENTS

Sunflower oil, for deep-frying

2 250g huss fillets, skinned

50g plain flour

2 eggs, lightly beaten

2 large handfuls white breadcrumbs

Homemade tartare sauce (see page 17)

● Preheat the sunflower oil to 180°C/350°F in a large pan or deep-fat fryer.

● Cut the huss fillets into finger-width strips. Season the flour with sea salt and spread it out on a large plate. Place the beaten eggs in a shallow bowl next to this, and lay out the breadcrumbs on a plate alongside the eggs.

● Take each piece of huss and coat it with the flour. Then dip it into the eggs and roll in the breadcrumbs till thoroughly covered.

● Carefully add the strips of fish, a few at a time, to the hot oil. Fry for 2–3 minutes, until golden-brown. Remove and place on a piece of kitchen paper to absorb excess oil, and keep hot on a pre-warmed dish. Reheat the oil before putting in each fresh batch of fish.

● When all the pieces are cooked, garnish with salad and serve hot with the homemade tartare sauce.

BAKED PLAICE WITH CRAYFISH & HERB BUTTER

SERVES 2

One of the most distinctive fish to be found off the Dorset coast, plaice can easily be identified by their orange spots. We're very used to seeing them at The Hive as they're brought in from the waters directly in front of the café (look out for the fishermen's flags fluttering above the sea, which mark the best catching grounds), so freshness is never an issue when they arrive in the kitchen. The delicate flesh responds well to roasting or baking, and makes a delicious contrast to the firmer, saltier crayfish tails in this recipe. Serve it with plenty of new potatoes to mop up the butter.

INGREDIENTS

2 whole 500–600g plaice, gutted
Olive oil
60g crayfish tails, roughly chopped
1 bunch parsley, roughly chopped

1 bunch dill, roughly chopped
1 bunch chives, roughly chopped
150g butter
1 lemon, zested and juiced

- Preheat the oven to 180°C/350°F.
- Put the plaice onto a baking tray, then drizzle with olive oil, sprinkle with sea salt and bake for 10–15 minutes, until cooked through.
- While the fish is cooking, prepare the crayfish and herb butter. Add the crayfish tails, parsley, dill and chives to the butter, then throw in the lemon zest and half the lemon juice. Mix well so all the ingredients are combined.
- Remove the plaice from the oven and place a generous portion of crayfish and herb butter on top.
- Put the fish back into the oven for 1 minute or until all the butter has melted, then serve.

LESLEY WATERS' GLAZED LEMON SOLE TART

SERVES 4

This wonderfully summery tart – perfect served with a light, freshly dressed salad – is one of the finest ways we've found to bring out the sweet, delicate flavour of lemon sole.

INGREDIENTS

250g shortcrust pastry

225g lemon sole fillet

300ml milk

1 bay leaf

25g butter

1 small onion, finely chopped

25g plain flour

1 egg, separated

Handful fresh parsley, chopped

Squeeze lemon juice

Homemade Hollandaise sauce (see page 16)

● Preheat the oven to 200°C/400°F. On a lightly floured surface, roll out the pastry and use to line a 20cm loose-bottomed tart tin. Chill for 15 minutes.

● Place greaseproof paper over the pastry and top with baking beans. Bake in the oven for 10–15 minutes. Remove the paper and beans, and return the tart case to the oven for 3–5 minutes until it is just cooked. Remove from the oven and reduce the heat to 180°C/375°F.

● Place the fish in a shallow pan and cover with the milk. Add the bay leaf and bring to the boil. Reduce the heat and poach very gently for 4–5 minutes or until the fish is just cooked.

● Remove the fish from the pan and allow to cool slightly, then coarsely flake. Reserve the cooking liquid and allow to cool.

● Heat the butter in a small pan. Add the onion and cook for 5–6 minutes until softened.

● Add the flour and cook, stirring for 1 minute. Remove from the heat and gradually stir in the cooled cooking liquid. Return the pan to the heat, bring to the boil and simmer for 2 minutes. Season the sauce and allow to cool slightly.

● Add the egg yolk, fish, parsley and lemon juice. Whisk the egg white to medium-stiff peak and gently fold in. Pour the mixture into the pastry case and bake for 20–25 minutes until set.

● Meanwhile, heat the grill to a medium-high setting and prepare the Hollandaise sauce. Spoon the sauce over the cooked tart and place it under the grill until browned. Serve at once.

PEPPERED SARDINES WITH SEA SALT

SERVES 2

Fresh sardines couldn't be further from the canned, tomato-slathered variety in terms of taste, and this simple recipe is an excellent showcase for their strong flavour. During the summer months, sardines are plentiful off Devon and Cornwall and, as we are situated just a few miles along the south coast, they inevitably find their way into our kitchen. Anyone eating this dish at The Hive on a hot day – especially when they're enjoying it with a hunk of bread and an ice-cold beer – could close their eyes and imagine they were in the Mediterannean. We often do…

INGREDIENTS

8 sardines, gutted and scaled
Olive oil

1 lemon, halved

● Place the sardines onto a roasting tray. Drizzle with olive oil, and sprinkle with sea salt and black pepper.
● Put the sardines under a hot grill for 4–5 minutes, until cooked through.
● Once cooked, remove the sardines from the grill and squeeze the lemon generously over them. Serve immediately, before they have a chance to cool.

AUTUMN

DOVER SOLE WITH A SHRIMP & CAPER BUTTER

SERVES 2

Dover sole may be one of the more expensive flatfish on the market, but its deliciously sweet, mild flavour makes it worth every penny. Unlike most other fish, it's best eaten a couple of days after catching, as its fine, firm-textured flesh tends to go a little tough when cooked too soon. And, here at The Hive, we believe that simplicity is key when preparing it. This straightforward, unfussy recipe, which throws only salty shrimps and the taste of herbs and lemon into the mix, allows the flavour of the fish to speak for itself. And very eloquent it is too...

INGREDIENTS

1 large whole Dover sole, top skin removed
Olive oil
Butter
Handful capers

Large handful shrimps
Handful parsley, chopped
½ lemon, juiced

● Preheat your grill. Place the Dover sole onto an oiled and seasoned baking tray, then season the fish and drizzle with olive oil. Grill for a few minutes, until cooked through. Remove and set aside in a warm place.

● Warm the baking tray on which you cooked the fish over a low heat until hot.

● Melt a large knob of butter on the tray and heat until it begins to foam and take on a nut-brown colour. Add the capers (their acidity stops the butter from burning) and the shrimps. Cook for 1–2 minutes.

● Place the Dover sole onto a large prewarmed plate, then pour the shrimp and caper butter generously over the top. Sprinkle with parsley and lemon juice, and serve immediately.

OYSTERS ROCKEFELLER

SERVES 1

First created in New Orleans at the end of the 19th century and named after John D Rockefeller – the wealthiest man in the US at that time – because of their incredibly rich sauce, oysters Rockefeller are a great way of using up any herbs you have hanging around the kitchen. Served in the half-shell, the oysters are always topped with breadcrumbs and grilled, but whatever else goes into the sauce is pretty much up to you. Here at The Hive, we've even been known to throw in ingredients we've foraged on trips along the clifftops and hedgerows around Burton Bradstock.

INGREDIENTS

12 oysters
Handful breadcrumbs
1 small white onion, sliced
Handful parsley, chopped
Handful chervil, chopped

Handful tarragon, chopped
Soft butter
Tabasco sauce
Rock salt

● Preheat your grill. Shuck the oysters according to the instructions on page 14, ensuring you retain the bottom part of the shell.
● Put the breadcrumbs, onion, parsley, chervil and tarragon into a food processor, and blitz until the mixture reaches as fine a consistency as possible. Add a generous knob of soft butter, a few drops of Tabasco sauce, and season with sea salt and black pepper. Mix well and set aside.
● Preheat your grill. On a baking tray, arrange the oysters on a bed of rock salt so they sit upright. Cover each with a spoonful of the breadcrumb mixture.
● Grill the oysters until the butter in the breadcrumb mixture starts to bubble and turn golden-brown. Be careful not to overcook.
● Serve straight from the salted baking tray.

BRILL WITH SAUTÉED WILD MUSHROOMS

SERVES 2

A lovely, chocolate-brown flatfish that's part of the turbot family, brill tastes every bit as good as its name suggests. Widely available in the English Channel – and pretty much everywhere from the coast of Iceland down to the Mediterranean – between October and February, it has a fine texture and a slightly sweet flavour that lends itself perfectly to the rich, earthy taste of wild mushrooms. This simple recipe is ideal for chilly, late-autumn afternoons, and goes wonderfully with a cold bottle of crisp white wine.

INGREDIENTS

1 whole 800g–1kg brill, head removed, trimmed and cut in half lengthways
Olive oil
Butter

2–3 handfuls wild mushrooms
Dash white wine
Dash double cream
Handful parsley, chopped

● Preheat your oven to 180°C/350°F and warm up a grill. Place the brill onto a baking tray, then season and drizzle with olive oil.
● Grill the fish until it starts to colour, then place in the oven for around 8 minutes, until it has almost cooked through. The brill will continue to cook for another 5 minutes when it's taken out of the oven, so you want it to be slightly underdone.
● While the fish is cooking, preheat a frying pan until hot. Add a knob of butter and a drizzle of olive oil, then sauté the mushrooms for a few minutes until they start to colour.
● Pour in the white wine and reduce by half, then add the cream and reduce the liquid until the sauce reaches a thick consistency. Remove from the heat and sprinkle with the parsley.
● Arrange the creamy wild mushroom sauce on a large plate and place the cooked brill on top. Serve while hot.

SURF CLAM CHOWDER

SERVES 2

This warming New England-style dish works very well in the old country, too. Especially on days when the temperature outside is a little bracing, and the ingredients used are fresh from the sea. At The Hive, we serve up several variations of this classic soup, depending on what our suppliers have brought us on that particular day, but we've found that surf clams – which we source from the Cornish coast – take it to another level.

INGREDIENTS

16 surf clams

1 leek, thinly sliced

Butter

Olive oil

4 large potatoes, diced

2 glasses white wine

2 cups milk

2 cups double cream

100g pancetta, cut into lardons

Handful chives, chopped

● Wash the clams in cold water and discard any that do not close when tapped.

● Sweat the leek along with a knob of butter and a little olive oil in a heavy-based pan over a medium heat until soft, then add the potatoes and season with a little sea salt.

● Warm the potatoes through for a couple of minutes then add 1 glass of white wine. Cover and cook for 5 minutes.

● Add in the milk and double cream in equal amounts until the potatoes are just covered. Replace the lid and cook for a few minutes. The potatoes are ready when you insert a thin knife into them and they slip off easily.

● While the potatoes are cooking, fry the pancetta in a pan until golden-brown. Remove and place on a piece of kitchen paper to soak up any excess oil. Set aside in a warm place.

● Pour a glass of white wine into another heavy-based saucepan then add the surf clams, and cover and steam until all have opened. Discard any that remain closed. Remove the meat from each with a small knife and set aside in a warm place. Retain the cooking liquor.

● Once the potatoes have cooked, set a few aside for garnishing. Then, with a hand blender, combine the remaining potatoes, cream and milk until the mixture is smooth. Season to taste, then add the clam meat, pancetta and enough retained cooking liquor to give the soup a creamy consistency.

● Garnish with potatoes and chives, and serve immediately with crusty bread.

TEMPURA HERRING ROE SALAD

SERVES 1

Herring roe – known colloquially as poor man's caviar – appears far more regularly in Asian, Mediterranean and Scandinavian cuisine than it does on British tables, which is a real shame as it is delicious, nutritious and incredibly good value. Its soft, creamy texture and smooth, delicate flavour may be criminally underrated, but this recipe – which wraps its distinctive taste in a light, crispy tempura batter – aims to redress that. We recommend you use clean oil to achieve the right level of crunchiness.

INGREDIENTS

Sunflower oil, for deep-frying
2 cups plain flour
1 cup cornflour
1 tbsp baking powder
150ml sparkling water

4–5 ice cubes
100g herring roe
Squeeze lemon juice
2 handfuls rocket leaves, to serve

● Preheat the sunflower oil to 180°C/350°F in a large pan or deep-fat fryer.
● Whisk together 1 cup plain flour with the cornflour, baking powder, sparkling water and ice cubes until the batter reaches the consistency of double cream. Don't worry if the ice cubes retain their shape. Set aside.
● Spread out the remaining plain flour and plenty of sea salt in a shallow dish, then coat lumps of the herring roe thoroughly in the mixture.
● Dip the herring roe into the batter, ensuring they are fully covered, and deep-fry until they start to colour and float to the surface. Cook for a further 1–2 minutes, then remove with chopsticks or tongs and place on a piece of kitchen paper to absorb the excess oil.
● Season with a squeeze of lemon, and a little sea salt and freshly ground pepper. Serve immediately with freshly dressed rocket leaves.

OUR SUPPLIERS: BRETT HIBBITT, WEYMOUTH

'I've got two strings to my bow,' says Brett Hibbitt of Jurassic Fishing in Weymouth. 'I run the boat as a charter craft, so I take people out on fishing trips, but I also do commercial fishing. I go out aiming for seabass mainly, but I also get things like pollock, cod, turbot, brill and bream. It's all rod-and-line caught, so it's very sustainable and eco-friendly, which is why The Hive deal with me a lot. They know it's all good fish.

'Between 80 to 90 per cent of my bass fishing is done within 10 miles of Weymouth. We do go a lot further sometimes, but you've got to be sure the fish are there because there's a lot of fuel to waste if they're not. We pick a spot where we think there's fish and we drift. We stop the boat uptide and drift down, everyone with a fishing rod and tackle. And if they're not there, you try somewhere else. Quite often, we're fishing in the Race off Portland, which is a very rough patch of water, so it gets a bit dicey sometimes. There have been accidents out there – a couple of boats have sunk over the years – but, if you're sensible enough, you stay out of the Race when it's dangerous and go in when it's just about doable.

'As soon we catch fish, it gets bled out, then put straight onto ice. I call The Hive from out at sea when I've finished my day's fishing and say, "I'll be there within the next hour, so let me know if you want anything." I bring the boat into Weymouth Harbour, land the fish, put it in the van and drive it down. Sometimes the fish is at The Hive within a couple of hours, ready to sell and be cooked.

'It's great to sell fish to The Hive as they get it out of the door quickly, so everyone knows it's really fresh. They've got four cracking chefs down there, too, who know how to cook a good fish meal. And they pass all the compliments they get about the bass onto me.'
Brett Hibbitt, 17 Southview Road, Weymouth (07916 129939; www.jurassicfishing.co.uk).

SCALLOPS WITH BOUDIN NOIR & PEA PURÉE

SERVES 2

Though hand-dived scallops aren't always available from Lyme Bay, their succulent flesh means we at The Hive go out of our way to get our hands on them as soon as the water's clear enough for gathering. This recipe, which teams their wonderfully delicate flavour with the dense, grainy taste of boudin noir – or black pudding to you and me – and deliciously fresh pea purée, is a real autumn treat. Ask your butcher to recommend you a really good boudin noir; the depth of flavour it provides is worth any additional expense.

INGREDIENTS

Dash chicken stock

200g peas

Butter

Dash double cream

200g boudin noir, cut into 8 chunks

8 scallops

Olive oil

2 handfuls salad leaves, to garnish

● Bring a pan of water and the chicken stock up to a rapid boil. Add the peas and simmer for 5 minutes until cooked.

● Drain the peas and blitz in a food processor until the mixture reaches a chunky consistency. Add a generous knob of butter, the double cream, and season well with sea salt and freshly ground black pepper. Mix and set aside in a warm place.

● Preheat your grill. Place the boudin noir chunks onto an oiled and seasoned baking tray, then grill for 1–2 minutes until slightly crispy. Set aside in a warm place.

● Place a heavy-bottomed pan onto a high heat. Lightly season the scallops and drizzle them with a little olive oil, then add to the pan.

● Sear the scallops on each side for 45–60 seconds (depending on their size), ensuring they're golden-brown where they've been in contact with the pan. Remove and place on a piece of kitchen paper to absorb the excess oil.

● Dot the pea purée around 2 plates and arrange the scallops on top. Fill in any gaps with the grilled chunks of boudin noir and garnish with fresh salad leaves. Serve immediately.

CREVETTE PRAWNS IN A SWEET & STICKY CHILLI SAUCE

SERVES 2

Though we at The Hive are dedicated to cooking with locally sourced ingredients wherever possible – and a huge proportion of the fish and seafood we prepare comes from within a few miles of Burton Bradstock – we make an exception when it comes to crevette prawns. These delicious shellfish, caught off the French coast, and boiled and flash-frozen on the boats, have a wonderful fresh flavour, and taste stunning when accompanied by this sweet, sticky chilli sauce. Be warned, this is a very messy meal. Make sure you've got fingerbowls and serviettes to hand.

INGREDIENTS

Olive oil
750g large crevette prawns
1 lemon, cut into wedges
1 tbsp paprika

Dash white wine
Bottle sweet chilli sauce
Handful chives, chopped

● Preheat a large frying pan until smoking-hot. Add a drizzle of olive oil, then put in the crevette prawns and lemon wedges.

● Cook for around 1 minute, stirring continually, until the prawn shells start to colour. Add the paprika and stir until evenly distributed around the pan, then pour in the white wine.

● When the liquid has reduced slightly (this will only take a few seconds), add several good glugs of the sweet chilli sauce. Turn the heat down and reduce the liquid until the sauce reaches a sticky consistency.

● Gently stir in the chopped chives, then serve immediately with chips or crusty bread.

HOMECURED GRAVLAX

SERVES 2

This Scandinavian dish has a very simple etymology. Its name comes from combining 'lax' or 'laks' – the Norse word for salmon – with 'grav', which means 'to dig' in Swedish, Norwegian and Danish. Burying food and curing it in the ground is a popular way to boost flavour in the lands up near the Arctic Circle but, thankfully, this recipe only requires you to inter your salmon in a mixture of sea salt, brown sugar and herbs. Usually served as a starter with thinly sliced bread and wedges of lemon or – if you want to continue the Nordic theme – some pickled cucumbers and rye bread, gravlax makes an indulgent autumn treat.

INGREDIENTS

1kg salmon fillet, gutted and pin-boned
100g sea salt
100g brown sugar
2 tbsp whole black peppercorns

1 tbsp English mustard
1 bunch dill, chopped
Dash brandy
Dash vodka

● Place the salmon fillet onto a chopping board and pat dry with kitchen paper. Line a deep baking tray with Clingfilm and place the salmon fillet, skin side down, on top.
● To prepare the curing mixture, combine the sea salt, brown sugar, peppercorns, mustard, dill, brandy and vodka in a large bowl.
● Sprinkle the curing mixture generously over the salmon, then lightly wrap the fish in the Clingfilm. Put a heavy weight, such as a chopping board, on top and place in the fridge for 24–48 hours.
● Once cured, serve in thin slices.

LOBSTER BISQUE

SERVES 2

This classic soup has its origins in France, where it became a way for those living in poor fishing communities to eke out every last bit of flavour from shellfish – even grinding up the shells to thicken the broth. We don't quite go that far at The Hive, but we believe that a thick, creamy soup, packed with the taste of the sea, is the very least our customers should expect. Lobster bisque is incredibly popular at the café during the autumn months and this smooth version, with its subtle hint of brandy – not to mention its delicious aroma of freshly cooked lobster – usually sells out as fast as we can make it.

INGREDIENTS

1 whole 750–1kg cooked lobster
Butter
1 medium onion, finely chopped
Blade mace
1 garlic clove, finely chopped
1 carrot, diced
1 bay leaf
3 sprigs thyme

200g good-quality tinned chopped tomatoes
Dash brandy
Dash white wine
50ml double cream
750ml fish stock (see page 15), or liquid left from boiling lobsters
Handful parsley, chopped

● Remove the meat from the lobster according to the instructions on page 13, then roughly chop and set aside.

● Melt a small knob of butter in a heavy-based casserole dish, then sauté the onion, mace, garlic, carrot, bay leaf and thyme for 5–10 minutes, stirring occasionally, until soft. Pour in the tomatoes and brandy, and cook for another 5 minutes.

● Add the lobster meat to the casserole dish, but keep some claw meat back to garnish.

● Increase the heat to medium-high and pour in the white wine and double cream. When the mixture starts to bubble, reduce the heat to low and cover. Cook for 10 minutes.

● Pour in the fish stock or the liquid in which you boiled the lobster, and take out the bay leaf and thyme.

● Purée the soup with a hand blender and strain it through a muslin gauze. Add in a small knob of butter and return to the stove to warm through. Season to taste.

● Serve garnished with the parsley and the reserved claw meat.

PAN-FRIED HUSS WITH CHINESE FIVE SPICE

SERVES 2

Despite its unfamiliar name, huss is better-known to fish-eaters than you might imagine. It also goes under the name of dogfish and, for years, it was branded as rock salmon and became a staple of the fish-and-chip shop menu until usurped by cheap North Atlantic cod in the 1970s. A cheap and plentiful alternative to scarcer, more expensive varieties of white fish, it takes on chilli and other spices fantastically well. And this simple recipe, which throws in the flavours of ground star anise, fennel seeds, cloves, cinnamon and Sichuan pepper, gives it a fabulously exotic Oriental twist.

INGREDIENTS

Jar Chinese five spice

1 good-sized huss fillet, cut into

3–5cm medallions

Butter

Olive oil

1 lemon, cut into wedges

● Preheat your oven to 180°C/350°F. Lay out the Chinese five spice in a dish then put in the huss medallions, one at a time, and coat evenly. Shake off any excess spice and set aside.

● Melt a knob of butter with a drizzle of olive oil in a shallow, non-stick frying pan. Turn the heat down to medium so as not to burn the spice, and fry the coated huss medallions until they start to colour. Turn over and repeat, then bake for 3–4 minutes in the oven. Keep the frying pan hot.

● Remove from the oven and return to the frying pan. Cook until the spicy coating is crisp.

● Serve with lemon wedges and fresh salad leaves.

MUSSELS IN A RED WINE, THYME & TOMATO SAUCE

SERVES 2

Though white wine is usually used when cooking mussels, we've found that red wine accompanies them just as well – and transforms the dish into something much more warming and comforting. The deeper, denser flavour and intense red colour somehow seem more appropriate during the autumn months. And – if our customers at The Hive are anything to go by – a big, steaming bowl of this deliciously succulent shellfish, flecked with herbs and served with warm, crusty bread or a portion of chips, proves very welcome indeed when the sky is leaden and the wind starts to swirl.

INGREDIENTS

900g mussels
1 onion, diced
Olive oil
1 garlic clove, finely chopped
Sprig thyme

1 bay leaf
Glass red wine
400g good-quality tinned chopped tomatoes
Handful parsley, chopped

● Wash the mussels in cold water and discard any that do not close when tapped.
● Preheat a large lidded saucepan and sweat the onion with a drizzle of olive oil until soft. Add the garlic, thyme and bay leaf, and cook for 1 minute.
● Add the mussels and cook for 1 minute, then add the red wine and cook until the liquid has reduced by half. Pour in the tomatoes, then cover and cook for around 3 minutes, shaking the sealed pan occasionally, until the mussels have opened. Discard any that remain closed.
● Sprinkle with parsley, divide between 2 bowls and serve immediately with a large glass of red wine.

MACKEREL WITH NEW POTATOES & TAPENADE

SERVES 2

Mackerel are plentiful in Lyme Bay from June right through to October each year so, at The Hive, we've never had a problem getting our hands on this beautiful, strong-flavoured fish. By autumn, though, the mackerel are starting to build up the fat reserves they need to get them through the winter, which means they taste all the better. This recipe, which teams their delicate, oily flesh with the healthy, vibrant flavour of olives and the last new potatoes of the season, is as easy as it is delicious.

INGREDIENTS

Handful pitted black olives

2 garlic cloves

4 anchovy fillets

1 tbsp capers

Squeeze lemon juice

Olive oil

8 new potatoes

8 mackerel fillets

Handful parsley, chopped

1 lemon, cut into wedges

● First, prepare the tapenade. Put the olives, garlic, anchovies, capers, lemon juice and a good dash of olive oil into a food processor, and add a little freshly ground black pepper. Blitz until thoroughly mixed, then set aside.

● Bring a pan of salted water up to the boil, then add the new potatoes. They are ready when you insert a thin knife into them and they slip off easily. Set aside in a warm place.

● Preheat your grill. Place the mackerel fillets onto an oiled and seasoned baking tray. Season the fish and drizzle with olive oil, then grill until cooked through.

● Warm a little olive oil in a saucepan over a medium heat. Add the cooked new potatoes and crush them with a fork while continually moving them around the pan.

● Once the potatoes are crushed and warmed through, pour in enough tapenade to bring the mixture together. Mix with the parsley.

● Divide the crushed new potatoes and tapenade between 2 dishes, then arrange the mackerel fillets on top. Garnish with lemon wedges and serve.

BAKED HALIBUT STEAKS WITH A HAZELNUT CRUST

SERVES 2

A truly enormous flatfish, the halibut is found in great numbers off the Dorset coast during the autumn months, and our suppliers regularly deliver us specimens that weigh 50 kilos or more. Its firm flesh and delicate taste lends itself to many cooking styles and, here at The Hive, we often serve up fillets in a light tempura batter. This recipe, though, is designed to show off the halibut's flavour with as few distractions as possible. The lovely, seasonal crust simply adds crunch and is the ideal complement to the clean, clear taste of the fish.

INGREDIENTS

2 250g halibut steaks

Olive oil

100g hazelnuts, toasted and crushed

1 egg

Small bunch parsley, chopped

50g melted butter

100g breadcrumbs

2 lemons, zested and juiced

● Preheat your oven to 180°C/350°F. Place the halibut steaks onto an oiled and seasoned baking tray, then season and drizzle with olive oil.

● Combine the hazelnuts, egg, parsley, melted butter, breadcrumbs, lemon zest and the juice of 1 lemon in a food processor or bowl. Mix well.

● Generously sprinkle the hazelnut mixture over the halibut steaks, then bake for 8–12 minutes, until cooked through.

● Serve straight from the oven with lemon wedges and a cold glass of white wine.

CUTTLEFISH STEW

SERVES 2

There's no point pretending that preparing cuttlefish isn't a labour-intensive task. Its inkiness means there's a good chance you – and your kitchen – will get very messy indeed and, because of this, many fishmongers choose not to stock it. Seeking out one who does, though, is well worth it. When thinly sliced and slow-cooked, such as in this delicious autumnal recipe, the octopus-like flesh of cuttlefish becomes wonderfully tender and forms the perfect base for a warming autumn stew. To avoid as much mess as possible, ask your fishmonger to clean and prepare the cuttlefish for you.

INGREDIENTS

Butter
1 red onion, roughly chopped
1 red pepper, roughly chopped
1 garlic clove
Small handful capers
Small handful anchovies

1 cuttlefish, thinly sliced
Dash white wine
Dash white wine vinegar
Pinch saffron
Handful vine-on cherry tomatoes
Handful parsley, chopped

● Melt a knob of butter in a large sauté pan, and gently sweat the red onion, red pepper, garlic, capers and anchovies until soft.
● Add the cuttlefish and cook for around 3 minutes, then pour in the white wine and white wine vinegar, and reduce the liquid by half.
● Put the saffron and tomatoes in, and simmer over a low heat for around 90 minutes, until the cuttlefish becomes tender. Sprinkle with parsley and serve while hot.

SMOKED HADDOCK RAREBIT WITH ROASTED TOMATOES

SERVES 2

Our Dorset take on the rustic Welsh classic, this recipe combines the dense flavours of smoked haddock with the bite of mustard and strong cheddar to stunning effect. It's perfect for those autumn lunchtimes when you need to banish the chill outside.

INGREDIENTS

4 tomatoes

Olive oil

300ml milk

1 bay leaf

1 tsp peppercorns

250g natural smoked haddock fillets, skinned and pin-boned

30g butter

30g plain flour

25g strong cheddar

2 egg yolks

1 tsp English mustard

Splash Worcestershire sauce

½ lemon, juiced

Handful parsley, chopped

2 slices granary bread

Bunch watercress, washed

● Preheat your oven to 180°C/350°F. Cut the tomatoes in half and place onto a roasting tray, then drizzle with olive oil and season. Place on a low oven shelf to roast until soft.

● Warm a saucepan, then add the milk, bay leaf, peppercorns and smoked haddock. Bring the mixture up to the boil and simmer for 5 minutes until the haddock has cooked through. Remove the fish from the pan and set aside. Make sure you retain the cooking liquor.

● Melt the butter in a saucepan, then add the flour and cook for 1 minute. Pour in the retained cooking liquor in stages, stirring continually, until the sauce reaches a smooth consistency.

● Simmer the sauce for around 5 minutes then remove from the heat and add the cheese, egg yolks, mustard, Worcestershire sauce, lemon juice, parsley and freshly ground black pepper. Mix in the smoked haddock. Set aside in the fridge.

● When the mixture has cooled, preheat a grill. Toast the granary bread, then coat each slice generously in the haddock-and-cheese mixture, and grill until golden-brown.

● Serve immediately with the roasted tomatoes and watercress.

RED MULLET WITH HOMEMADE PESTO

SERVES 2

A staple of Mediterranean seafood cookery, red mullet eschews the warm waters of the Italian and Greek coasts in autumn and heads in great numbers for Dorset. Though the fish can be relatively expensive, its punchy flavour makes it a very worthwhile purchase – especially for those for whom seafront summer-holiday meals still linger in the memory. At The Hive, we like to team its fine and delicate texture with the fresh and fiery taste of homemade pesto. And, as we prepare this in the traditional Ligurian way, we like to think it makes the red mullet feel very much at home.

INGREDIENTS

125g fresh basil, chopped
1 garlic clove, minced
65g parmesan, grated
100g toasted pine nuts
225ml extra-virgin olive oil

4 250g red mullet fillets, scaled and pin-boned
2 handfuls wild rocket leaves
1 lemon, cut into wedges

● First, prepare the homemade pesto. Put the basil, garlic, parmesan and pine nuts into a food processor, and add in half the olive oil. Blitz together, and continue adding oil until the mixture reaches a smooth consistency, similar to that of double cream.

● Place the red mullet fillets onto an oiled and seasoned baking tray. Season the fish and drizzle with olive oil, then place under a moderate grill until cooked through.

● Divide the wild rocket between 2 prewarmed plates and lay the fillets on top. Drizzle generously with the homemade pesto and serve immediately with lemon wedges and a glass of dry white wine.

CHILLI CRAB LINGUINE

SERVES 2

Occupying a place somewhere between spaghetti and fettucine in the pasta spectrum, linguine originated in Campania, southern Italy, where it proved the ideal accompaniment to the fish and seafood sauces so typical of that region. Its long, flat strands work particularly well with the soft, sweet-tasting meat from crabs that are still readily available along the south coast in autumn. And, though this simple recipe has its roots in Tyrrhenian climes, its spiciness – which you can pep up by simply adding more chilli – is perfectly suited to a misty Dorset afternoon.

INGREDIENTS

1 medium-hot red chilli, deseeded and finely chopped
1 fat garlic clove, finely chopped
3 pared strips lemon zest, finely chopped
Olive oil
450g linguine

2 tbsp lemon juice
225g freshly cooked white and brown crab meat (see page 13)
2 tbsp fresh flat-leaf parsley, chopped
1 spring onion, chopped
1 lemon, cut into wedges

● Put the chilli, garlic, lemon zest and 100ml of olive oil into a small pan and cook over a gentle heat until it begins to sizzle. Remove from the heat and set aside.

● Bring a large saucepan of well-salted water up to the boil. Add the linguine and cook for 8–9 minutes (check the packet instructions), or until al dente. Drain well and set aside.

● Pour the chilli, garlic, lemon zest and olive oil mixture into the pan in which you cooked the pasta, then add the lemon juice, and season with sea salt and freshly ground black pepper.

● Heat the mixture until it begins to sizzle, then add the linguine and crab meat to the pan. Toss gently over a medium heat until the crab meat has warmed through.

● Add the parsley and spring onion, and season well with sea salt and freshly ground black pepper. Drizzle with olive oil and serve immediately with lemon wedges on the side.

LESLEY WATERS' RAINBOW TROUT FISHCAKES

SERVES 4

One of the few fish included in this book that couldn't be described as seafood, the rainbow trout – found in freshwater lakes and streams – is well worth making an exception for. This delicious recipe from our friend Lesley Waters showcases its delicate flavour and firm texture in a classic lunchtime dish.

INGREDIENTS

500g Maris Piper potatoes, peeled
480g rainbow trout fillets
250ml milk
25g butter
1 packet flat-leaf parsley, chopped
½ packet chives, chopped
1 cup plain flour

1 egg, beaten
115g fresh white breadcrumbs
Sunflower oil, for frying
115g French beans, trimmed, blanched
and refreshed
115g baby spinach leaves
Homemade rocket salsa verde (see page 17)

● Cut the potatoes into chunks and place in a saucepan. Cover them with water and bring to the boil. Add half a teaspoon of salt and simmer gently for 15 minutes until tender.
● Place the fish in a large shallow pan; pour over the milk and cover. Bring to the boil and simmer very gently for 5–6 minutes or until the fish is just cooked. Remove the fish with a slotted spoon and leave to cool on a plate. Remove the skin and roughly flake the fish.
● Drain the potatoes and mash with the butter.
● In a large bowl, mix together the mash, parsley and chives, and season generously with salt and pepper. Gently fold in the flakes of fish.
● Using floured hands, shape the mixture into 4 round cakes. Dip each into the egg followed by the breadcrumbs. Chill for up to 24 hours.
● Heat the oil in a large frying pan and shallow-fry the cakes over a medium heat for 3–4 minutes on each side until golden-brown and completely heated through. Toss the beans and spinach together, divide onto 4 dinner plates and top with a fishcake. Serve with the homemade rocket salsa verde and lemon wedges.

TURBOT WITH BLACKEYED BEAN CASSOULET

SERVES 2

Even though it's in season between September and February, the turbot certainly couldn't be described as plentiful. Its appearance in The Hive's kitchen is the exception rather than the rule, and this is why we hold it in such high regard. The firm, sweet flesh makes it a beautiful eating fish – though we've found that a mid-sized turbot of around 1 kilo works best, as smaller ones tend to be too bony and the meat in the large specimens can often be a little too tough. This straightforward recipe dresses up its wonderful flavour with a few simple ingredients.

INGREDIENTS

Olive oil

2 small chorizo sausages, sliced

½ onion, diced

1 garlic clove, chopped

Pinch smoked paprika

400g good-quality tinned chopped tomatoes

400g tinned blackeyed beans, rinsed

500ml chicken stock

1 sprig thyme

1 bay leaf

1 whole 1kg turbot, filleted

● Preheat your oven to 180°C/350°F. Warm a little olive oil in a large sauté pan and fry the chorizo until it starts to colour.

● Add the onion, garlic and smoked paprika, and cook until the onion is soft. Put in the tomatoes, blackeyed beans, chicken stock, thyme and bay leaf. Simmer for 40 minutes.

● Preheat your grill. Place the turbot fillets onto an oiled and seasoned baking tray, then season and drizzle with olive oil. Grill for a few minutes until the skin becomes slightly crispy, then bake in the oven for around 8 minutes, until cooked through.

● Check the seasoning in the cassoulet then pour it into a large serving dish. Arrange the cooked turbot fillets on top and serve while still hot.

KINGFISHER
MARKET ONLY
KINGFISHER
DIRECT SEAFOOD
BRIXHAM
KINGFISHER
FRIDGE ONLY

OUR SUPPLIERS: KINGFISHER BRIXHAM, DEVON

'Kingfisher Brixham began with Nick Summersby and his father Gordon,' says Cathy Dando, the company's southwest sales manager. 'They started supplying local pubs and restaurants in the Brixham area and then it grew. We now go as far up as Derby and right across to Brighton. The ethos hasn't changed, though. It's still all about quality fish landed locally.

'We're a family-owned business and even though we're now part of Seafood Holdings – a massive multinational organisation – they've left us very much as a standalone company. That's given us much greater buying power and we can now source fish from much further afield. We buy approximately 95 per cent of our stock from Brixham Market, but we have access to all the fish markets in the UK. If anyone wanted a red snapper, for example, we'd be able to get one in for them.

'It's traceablility that sets us apart. Customers such as The Hive can go online or phone our office, and see where their fish was landed and at what time. We can tell them the name of the skipper who caught it, roughly where he found it, and whether it was trawled or line-caught. We like to give our clients as much information as possible so they can pass it on to their customers. It's a good talking point.

'Most of our staff have been with us for a very long time. Brixham is a close community and obviously it's all based around the fishing industry, so we recruit locally. The majority of the guys who work for us had fathers and grandfathers in the fishing trade. They've grown up knowing fish and we want to keep it that way.'

Kingfisher Brixham, Unit 4–5 Torbay Business Park, Woodview Road, Paignton (01803 553232; www.kingfisherbrixham.co.uk).

RAZOR CLAMS WITH A LEMON & LIME VINAIGRETTE

SERVES 2

Freshness is everything when it comes to razor clams – so this recipe, which requires little more than plucking them from the sand and throwing them on the barbecue, guarantees an absolutely stunning flavour. A perfect dish for those warm, early autumn evenings when the sunlight hangs around just long enough for you to stay out on the beach, this combination of the clams' delicate flesh and the zesty citric zing of the easy-to-make vinaigrette is certain to impress those standing around the hot coals. Make sure you bring plenty of cold beers to wash them down with.

INGREDIENTS

10 razor clams, rinsed
Extra-virgin olive oil
3 lemons, juiced

1 lime, juiced
1 garlic clove, finely chopped
1 bunch coriander, chopped

● Preheat your barbecue until it's red-hot. Place the razor clams into a large bowl and drizzle with olive oil.
● In another bowl, mix the lemon and lime juice with the chopped garlic, coriander, and plenty of sea salt and freshly ground black pepper. Slowly add in half a cup of olive oil, whisking continually.
● Arrange the razor clams on top of the hot barbecue and cook them until they open. Drizzle generously with more olive oil and serve immediately in their shells with the vinaigrette spooned over the top.

SMOKED HADDOCK CHOWDER

SERVES 1

Another variation on the all-American classic, our haddock chowder is always made with naturally smoked haddock. We avoid anything that's been dyed, as we've found that it doesn't taste as good and – what with all the sweetcorn we include – there's a danger of too much yellow colouring the soup. At The Hive, we like to blitz only half of the corn so we get a rougher texture, but feel free to ignore this if you a prefer a smooth dish. The ideal recipe for a cold autumn afternoon, this is best served steaming-hot with lots of crusty bread to mop your bowl.

INGREDIENTS

1 onion, sliced

1 leek, finely sliced

4 rashers smoked bacon, cut into lardons

50g butter

1 Maris Piper potato, peeled and cubed

Glass white wine

300ml fish stock (see page 15)

2 bay leaves

250ml full-fat milk

200ml double cream

200g tinned sweetcorn, drained

450g smoked haddock, skinned and cubed

Handful parsley, chopped

● Sweat the onion, leek and bacon along with the butter in a heavy-based pan until soft.

● Add the potato, white wine, fish stock, bay leaves, milk and double cream, then bring to the boil and simmer until the potatoes are cooked. They are ready when you insert a thin knife into them and they slip off easily.

● Pour the sweetcorn into a food processor and blitz. At The Hive, we retain half the sweetcorn as we like a rough-textured chowder, but how much you choose to blitz depends on personal preference.

● Once the potatoes have cooked, add the sweetcorn and smoked haddock to the pan and simmer until the haddock has cooked through.

● Sprinkle with parsley, season to taste and serve immediately.

KIPPERS & SOFT POACHED EGGS ON GRANARY TOAST

SERVES 2

One of the staples of our autumn and winter breakfast menus, this dish has proved so phenomenally popular over the years that we find it hard to take it off during the warmer months. Kippers – or cold-smoked herrings – used to be ubiquitous on the breakfast table in the years before World War II, but have appeared less since the advent of packaged cereals. They're seen as more of a treat these days. But as kippers are so inexpensive and recipes such as this – which team their distinctive, oily flavour with the moreish yolkiness of soft-poached eggs – are so delicious, there's no reason why they can't mount a comeback.

INGREDIENTS

2 kippers, heads removed

Olive oil

Butter

Splash white wine vinegar

2 eggs

2 thick slices granary bread

2 handfuls watercress, washed

1 lemon, cut into wedges

● Preheat your grill. Place the kippers, skin side down, onto an oiled and seasoned baking tray, then season and drizzle with olive oil. Place a knob of butter on each one and grill until they are cooked through.

● While the kippers are cooking, bring a pan of water up to the boil, and add the white wine vinegar and a pinch of sea salt. Carefully crack in the eggs and poach for 2–3 minutes.

● Once the kippers have cooked, gently peel back the spine to remove all the bones in one go. Set aside in a warm place.

● Toast the granary bread and divide between 2 plates. Arrange the cooked kippers on top and finish with a poached egg and a handful of watercress. Serve immediately with lemon wedges.

OYSTERS & GUINNESS

SERVES 1

There's not much to this recipe – if, indeed, you can call it that at all – but its sheer simplicity is what makes it special. The briny tang of the oysters goes absolutely perfectly with the bitterness of the Guinness, and when it's all pepped up with the sharpness of freshly squeezed lemon, you've got a dish that can more than hold its own alongside the fanciest of seafood creations. We use oysters from Devon's River Yealm at The Hive, as the food miles involved are minimal and we can be assured of their freshness, but, so long as you get hold of ones reared as near to you as possible, they'll taste pretty fabulous. The Guinness, as any Irishman will tell you, should be draught-pulled or in a bottle – certainly not in a can.

INGREDIENTS

6 oysters
1 lemon, cut into 6 wedges

600ml (1 pint) draught or bottled Guinness

- Shuck your oysters according to the instructions on page 14. Place on a dish (ideally over ice) and arrange the lemon wedges around them.
- Pour yourself a pint of Guinness and get stuck in.

TEMPURA BRILL WITH A CREAMY PANCETTA SAUCE

SERVES 2

An upmarket take on traditional fish and chips, this dish encases the light texture and subtly sweet taste of brill in a crispy, herb-flecked batter. Add to this the autumnal flavours of salty pancetta and fresh garden peas, infused throughout a warming, creamy sauce, and you've got a meal that's ideal for the cold afternoons toward the end of the season. Serve it with plenty of lemon wedges, bowls of hot, hand-cut chips and a cold bottle of sparkling wine.

INGREDIENTS

Sunflower oil, for deep-frying

3 cups plain flour

150ml sparkling water

2 handfuls parsley, finely chopped

3 slices pancetta, cut into lardons

Glass white wine

1 cup garden peas

Dash double cream

2 large brill fillets, scaled and pin-boned

Watercress, to garnish

● Preheat the sunflower oil to 180°C/350°F in a large pan or deep-fat fryer. You need to put in enough oil to fully cover the fish.

● Whisk together 2 cups of flour with the sparkling water to create a thin batter. Mix in 1 handful of chopped parsley and set aside.

● Preheat a pan and sauté the pancetta until golden-brown. Pour in the white wine and garden peas, and reduce by half; then add the double cream and reduce by half again. Sprinkle in the remaining parsley and set aside in a warm place.

● Spread out the remaining flour and plenty of sea salt on a baking tray, and coat the brill fillets thoroughly with the mixture.

● Dip the fillets into the batter, ensuring they are evenly covered, and deep-fry for a couple of minutes, until the batter is golden and the fish is cooked through. Use a pair of tongs to keep the fish moving in the oil so it doesn't stick.

● Divide the pancetta sauce between 2 plates, and place a small handful of watercress on top. Arrange the brill fillets over this and serve immediately with hot bowls of chips.

GRILLED GARFISH WITH LEMON ZEST, PARSLEY & OLIVE OIL

SERVES 2

Similar in taste and texture to the better-known sardine, garfish are plentiful off the south coast between June and October each year. Their fine, delicate flesh – not to mention their high fat content – makes them prime candidates for smoking and pickling, but at The Hive we like to serve them as simply as possible. This easy recipe, which teams the fish with a little grated lemon zest, a touch of parsley and a drizzle of good-quality olive oil (Filippo Berio or Sasso if you can get it), is the best way we've found to show off garfish's sweet and delicate flavour.

INGREDIENTS

8 garfish, gutted and scaled
Good-quality extra-virgin olive oil

2 lemons, 1 cut into wedges
Handful parsley, finely chopped

● Preheat a medium grill. Place the garfish onto a baking tray, then brush with a little olive oil and lightly season. Grill until cooked through.
● Evenly zest 1 lemon over the cooked garfish with a fine grater then divide the fish between 2 prewarmed plates.
● Garnish with parsley then drizzle generously with olive oil. Season with freshly ground black pepper and serve immediately with lemon wedges.

WINTER

HOT SHELLFISH RISOTTO

SERVES 2

Here at The Hive, we serve this bold and rustic dish in the pan in which it's cooked – which gives it a real wow-factor. We've found that leaving the shells on certainly improves the flavour of this recipe, but if you want to avoid messiness, then using shelled seafood is fine. Serve it with warm crusty bread and a glass of white wine.

INGREDIENTS

2 shallots, finely sliced

Butter

Olive oil

150g Arborio rice

1 tsp tomato purée

Splash brandy

Pinch saffron

Pinch smoked paprika

2 bay leaves

250ml tinned chopped tomatoes

250ml shellfish stock (see page 15)

1 cooked lobster, cut in half

4 king prawns

4 langoustines

10 mussels

4 scallops

Splash single cream

Handful flat-leaf parsley, chopped

2 lemons, cut into wedges

● First, sweat the shallots in a large pan with a knob of butter and a splash of olive oil, until soft. Next, put in the Arborio rice and cook for 1 minute; then add the tomato purée and cook for another couple of minutes.

● Add the brandy (be careful, this might flame), then the saffron, paprika, bay leaves, tinned tomatoes and a ladleful of shellfish stock. Stir until the rice has absorbed all the liquid, then continue adding the stock in stages, stirring regularly and waiting until the rice has absorbed it before adding more. Once all the stock has gone in, remove from the heat and set the risotto to one side.

● Preheat another large pan (the one in which you'll serve up in) and put in another knob of butter and a splash of olive oil. Add the cooked lobster, king prawns, langoustines, mussels and scallops, then cover and fry for 2–3 minutes, until the mussels start to open.

● Add the risotto and cream, and continue cooking for a few more minutes, until the shellfish is ready to eat. Season to taste and serve immediately, sprinkled with flat-leaf parsley and with a few lemon wedges on the side.

BAKED POUTING IN A CURRIED MUSSEL BROTH

SERVES 2

Pouting – a cheap and sustainable alternative to cod – works well with curry, as its firm texture and delicate flavour stand up to the spices. Whenever we cook this dish on a cold day at The Hive, the delicious aromas that come from the kitchen ensure a rush of orders.

INGREDIENTS

Half butternut squash, diced
Half sweet potato, diced
Olive oil
10 mussels
2 250g pouting fillets
1 onion, diced
1 red pepper, diced
Butter

1 garlic clove, chopped
Pinch saffron
Pinch curry powder
300ml fish stock (see page 15)
Splash white wine
Glass double cream
2 sprigs coriander

● Preheat your oven to 180°C/350°F. Spread out the diced butternut squash and sweet potato on a roasting tray, then drizzle generously with olive oil and season to taste. Roast for around 10 minutes, until soft.

● Wash the mussels in cold water and discard any that do not close when tapped.

● Place the pouting fillets onto another roasting tray, then drizzle with olive oil and season. Roast for 5–10 minutes, until cooked through.

● Sweat the onion and red pepper in a pan with a knob of butter and a splash of olive oil till soft. Then add the garlic, saffron and curry powder, and cook for around 1 minute. Put the mussels in the pan and fry for another minute before adding the fish stock and white wine.

● When the liquid has reduced by half, pour in the double cream and place a lid on the pan. Steam the mussels for 2–3 minutes until open. Discard any that remain closed.

● Once the mussels are cooked, add the roasted butternut squash and sweet potatoes to the broth, and warm it through. Spoon the curried mussel broth into 2 bowls and place a roasted pouting fillet on top of each. Garnish with a sprig of coriander and serve immediately.

WHITING GOUJONS WITH GUACAMOLE & CHILLI SALT

SERVES 2

Whiting may be a member of the cod family, but it is a cheaper and far more sustainable option than its somewhat over-fished bigger cousin. It has a similar sweet and delicate taste, but the flesh is less robust – so it's best to cook it quickly before it starts to break down. This dish does exactly that. The whiting strips spend only a short time in hot oil before they're ready to be dipped into delicious homemade guacamole and spicy chilli salt. Here at The Hive, we've been known to get them from sea to plate in just a few minutes.

INGREDIENTS

2 250g whiting fillets
Handful plain flour
2 eggs, beaten
Handful breadcrumbs
1 ripe avocado

½ red chilli
1 lemon, juiced
Sunflower oil, for deep-frying
Pinch dried chilli

● Slice the whiting fillets into thin, finger-width strips. Lay out three plates; plain flour on one, beaten eggs on another and breadcrumbs on the third.
● Roll the whiting strips in the flour, then the egg and, finally, the breadcrumbs. Once all are coated, set aside in the fridge. This can be done up to 24 hours in advance.
● Prepare the guacamole by first peeling and removing the stone from the avocado. Then blitz it in a food processor with the chilli and lemon juice, until it reaches the consistency of a rough paste.
● Preheat the sunflower oil to 180°C/350°F in a large pan or deep-fat fryer. Deep-fry the coated whiting strips until golden-brown and cooked through.
● Serve immediately with the homemade guacamole and a small bowl of sea salt mixed with dried chilli.

THE HIVE FISH PIE

SERVES 4

What's left to say about this fabulous winter classic? Everyone knows that succulent chunks of fish in a creamy sauce, topped with mashed potato and cheese, make the perfect meal when the weather is cold. That doesn't make it any less special though…

INGREDIENTS

4 eggs

1 onion

4 cloves

600ml full-fat milk

2 bay leaves

Pinch freshly grated nutmeg

2 sprigs thyme

400g cod fillet, skinned

400g salmon fillet, skinned and pin-boned

400g natural smoked haddock fillet, skinned and pin-boned

Handful parsley, chopped

1kg Maris Piper potatoes

100g butter

50g plain flour

50g strong cheddar, grated

● Preheat your oven to 200°C/400°F. Hard-boil the eggs by immersing them in boiling water for 8 minutes. Once cooked, put them into cold water to prevent the yolks from going grey.

● Next, cut the onion in half and stud one section with cloves. Put the studded half onion, milk, bay leaves, nutmeg and thyme into a pan along with all the fish. If it isn't completely covered, add more milk. Bring the mixture to the boil then reduce to a simmer for 8 minutes, until the fish has cooked through.

● Once the fish has been poached, lift it out onto a plate and break it into chunks. Place it into an oven dish, then de-shell the eggs and break them up over the top. Add chopped parsley, then mix and place the dish into the fridge for later. Strain the cooking liquor from the pan into a jug.

● Boil the potatoes till soft, then drain and add half the butter. Mash and set to one side.

● Pour the cooking liquor into a pan and bring to the boil. Melt the remaining butter in another pan, then add flour and stir till the mixture comes together. Pour in the boiling cooking liquor in stages and stir slowly until the sauce is smooth and all the milk has been added.

● Take the fish mixture out from the fridge and pour the sauce over the top. Top with mashed potatoes and grated cheese (we like to use Ashley Chase cheddar at The Hive), and place in the oven for about 20 minutes, until the fish pie is golden-brown and piping-hot throughout.

ROASTED COD WITH BUTTERED CABBAGE, PANCETTA & TOMATO

SERVES 2

A staple of our Christmas menu – and a lot more popular with customers at The Hive than roast turkey – this wonderful combination of firm, fresh cod with crisp pancetta and deliciously buttery cabbage is the perfect antidote to the plummeting winter temperatures. Though we usually make this dish with cod, it works just as well with pollock, salmon, sea trout or haddock. Try it with an ice-cold glass of white wine to cut through the strong, salty flavours.

INGREDIENTS

150g pancetta
2 250g cod fillets, scaled and pin-boned
Olive oil
2 tomatoes

Butter
Half Savoy cabbage, finely sliced
Small bunch chives, chopped

● Preheat your oven to 180°C/350°F. Cut two thin slices of pancetta, then arrange on a roasting tray and place in the oven for around 10 minutes. At The Hive, we always put another roasting tray on top of the pancetta while it cooks, as this helps keep it thin and crispy. Once done, set aside in a warm place.

● Place the cod fillets onto a roasting tray, then drizzle with olive oil and season. Roast for 10–15 minutes, until cooked through.

● While the fish is cooking, cut the tomatoes in half, then drizzle with a little olive oil and season to taste. Place on a low oven shelf to roast.

● Cut the remaining pancetta into lardons. Put a knob of butter into a pan and fry the pancetta and the Savoy cabbage until the cabbage has softened.

● Divide the pancetta and cabbage between 2 large bowls, and place a roasted cod fillet on top of each. Arrange the halves of tomato on the side and a slice of crispy pancetta on top. Sprinkle with chives, then serve.

BAKED SCALLOPS IN A CHEESE SAUCE

SERVES 2

This recipe – our take on the classic French dish Coquilles Saint-Jacques Mornay – is perfect comfort food. And the scallops, served in their shells, look amazing served either as a starter or main course. At The Hive, we use Lyme Bay scallops when possible and Ashley Chase cheese from Dorset's Bride Valley in the sauce, but if you source the ingredients carefully – ie, as locally as possible – then it should taste just as wonderful.

INGREDIENTS

10 scallops in their shells
4 Maris Piper potatoes, peeled and
chopped into cubes
Butter
White pepper

25g plain flour
600ml milk
1 tsp wholegrain mustard
80g strong cheddar, grated
Olive oil

● Preheat a grill and prepare the scallops according to the instructions on page 14. Retain the shells, though, and scrub them clean in readiness to serve the dish in.
● Put the potatoes into a pan and boil until soft, then remove from the heat and mash with a knob of butter and plenty of sea salt and white pepper. Set aside in a warm place.
● Melt 25g butter in a saucepan, then add the flour and cook for 1 minute. Stir in the milk in stages until the sauce has a smooth consistency. Simmer for 8–10 minutes, stirring continually, then mix in the mustard and half the grated cheese. Remove from the heat and set aside in a warm place.
● Warm another pan until it's smoking-hot. Coat the scallops in olive oil and season with sea salt and white pepper, then add them to the pan. Fry on each side for 1 minute, until the flesh turns a golden-brown colour. When the scallops are coloured all over, remove from the heat and set aside.
● Place the scallop shells onto a baking tray and arrange mashed potato into the bottom of each one. Add a scallop on top, cover with cheese sauce and finish with the remaining grated cheese.
● Grill until the scallops are golden-brown on top and piping-hot throughout. Serve immediately with a glass of cold white wine.

BRILL WITH A POACHED DUCK'S EGG & PANCETTA

SERVES 2

Fish for breakfast? It might be an unusual choice, but kippers have always gone down well with a cup of tea and the morning papers, so why not brill? This delicious combination of delicate, mildly sweet fillets, salty pancetta and rich duck's egg has flown off The Hive's winter breakfast menu in the run-up to this book's publication, and – as our customers tend to know a good thing when they see it – we absolutely had to include the recipe. Try it at home. It's a fabulous alternative to the usual breakfast options – and works just as well at lunchtime, too.

INGREDIENTS

Splash white wine vinegar
4 slices pancetta
2 large brill fillets, scaled and pin-boned
Olive oil

2 duck's eggs
Small handful chives, chopped
1 lemon, cut into wedges

● Preheat your grill. Bring a pan of water and the white wine vinegar up to the boil.
● Place the pancetta onto a roasting tray and grill until crispy. At The Hive, we always put another roasting tray on top of the pancetta while it cooks, as this helps it keep its shape and crisp evenly.
● Cut the brill fillets in half at an angle to give them a nice shape. Oil and season the fillets, and place them under the grill for around 2 minutes, until cooked through.
● While the fish is cooking, crack the duck's eggs into the boiling water and poach until the eggs hold their shape and the white is cooked (the yolk should still be runny).
● Divide the brill fillets between 2 plates, and top with a poached duck's egg and the crispy pancetta. Sprinkle with chives and serve immediately with a lemon wedge on the side.

OUR SUPPLIERS: WEYFISH, WEYMOUTH

'I've been on the quay all my life,' says Colin Horne (*right*) of fish market Weyfish in Weymouth, just along the Dorset coast from The Hive. 'I was born here. I served my apprenticeship on the paddle steamers and I fished as well. That's how we ended up here. My business partner Bob and I were fishermen, getting on in age, and we heard that the bloke who ran the town's only harbourside fish market was about to retire. "That's an opportunity," I said to Bob. "We ought to take it on because if it closes down, there'll be nothing here." So I came ashore, Bob came ashore, and we started on this. We've been here for 24 years now.

'We do everything from retail to wholesale supply for restaurants. We specialise in live shellfish, and export a lot of lobsters, crabs and spider crabs to Spain. We buy most of our stuff from local fishermen – though we take our crabs to Billingsgate Market up in London once a week and bring back more exotic fish such as snapper for the restaurants around here.

'We've been working with The Hive for years. We sell them a lot of crab meat, lobsters and our large cooked crabs because they do a huge family platter down there. Normally on a Friday, they'll ring us up and say, "We want 60 to 100 pounds of crab meat, and so many lobsters and whatever." They're good lads.

'I'm 74 now and it's time I retired. You come to a stage when you can't do what you used to do. But I'd want this place to stay as a fish market. It's the only one in the town. The lads who work the counter know all the customers by name; and people come in to have a laugh and joke with us. If this went, then so would the local touch. It'd be a tragedy; you'd have to go back to the supermarket.'

Weyfish, Old Fish Market, Custom House Quay, Weymouth (01305 761277).

THE HIVE HOT SHELLFISH PLATTER

SERVES 2

A real winter winner at The Hive, this gargantuan dish is as popular during the chillier months as its cold equivalent is during the summer. There's no real formula to creating it – we tend to use whatever's fresh and available in the kitchen on that day – but lobster, mussels, langoustines and clams are usually involved. There's no reason why you have to follow us to the letter on this one, though. Why not see what shellfish your fishmonger has on the counter when you visit, and take it from there? You can increase the overall spiciness by adding another chilli or two, too.

INGREDIENTS

1 cooked lobster, halved

1 handful mussels

1 handful clams

10 langoustines

10 king prawns

2 shallots, finely sliced

1 garlic clove, finely chopped

2 red chillies, finely chopped

Butter

Glass cava

Glass double cream

Handful parsley, chopped

1 lemon, cut into wedges

- Wash the mussels and clams in cold water, and discard any that do not close when tapped.
- Preheat a large pan and fry the shallots, garlic and chillies with a knob of butter until soft.
- Add the langoustines, mussels, king prawns and clams, then cover and steam for 1 minute. Put in the two lobster halves and cook for around 1 minute more.
- Pour in the cava and reduce by half, then add the cream and reduce again until the shellfish are hot throughout, and the mussels and clams have opened.
- Discard any mussels or clams that remain closed, then sprinkle with the parsley. Finish with a squeeze of lemon and serve the dish while still steaming.

SMOKED HADDOCK KEDGEREE

SERVES 2

This combination of spicy rice, fish and hard-boiled eggs is thought to have been brought to the UK by British colonials returning from Raj-era India. It has been gracing breakfast tables for hundreds of years now – though, at The Hive, we're just as likely to serve it at lunch or dinner. Simply add more curry powder if you want to up the heat levels.

INGREDIENTS

2 large eggs

500g naturally smoked haddock fillets, skinned and pin-boned

300ml milk

2 fresh bay leaves

170g long-grain or basmati rice

Butter

Thumb-sized piece of fresh ginger, peeled and grated

1 medium onion

1 garlic clove, finely chopped

2 heaped tbsp curry powder

1 tbsp mustard seeds

2 lemons, juiced

1 handful fresh coriander, chopped

1 red chilli, finely chopped

● Bring a pan of water to the boil and put the eggs in gently to prevent them cracking. Boil for 8 minutes, then place straight into cold water to prevent the yolks from going grey. Peel the eggs once they've cooled and set aside in the fridge.

● Put the smoked haddock and bay leaves in an oven-proof dish and add enough milk to cover. Bring to the boil, then cover and simmer for around 5 minutes, until the haddock has cooked through. Leave to cool, then remove the fish and set aside. Retain the cooking liquor.

● Boil the rice for 10 minutes until it's cooked, then strain and cool in cold water. Drain the rice once more and set aside in the fridge.

● In a pan, melt a knob of butter over a low heat. Add the ginger, onion and garlic, and cook until soft, then put in the curry powder and mustard seeds. Cook for a few minutes more, then add the rice and enough of the retained cooking liquor to thin the mixture slightly. Pour in the lemon juice.

● Cut the cooled eggs into quarters. Combine the cooked smoked haddock and the rice mixture in a large pan and heat through. Add the eggs, coriander and chilli, and stir gently.

● Divide between 2 bowls and serve.

LESLEY WATERS' GARLIC MUSSEL BISQUE

SERVES 2

This recipe, given to us by long-time friend of The Hive Lesley Waters, is one of our absolute favourites. On evenings when it's dark by 4pm and it's so cold outside that you can't feel your fingers when you venture through the door, this is the sort of meal you want on the table. The plump, meaty mussels are the perfect foil for the thick tomatoey sauce and the sweet, aromatic garlic, and it positively demands to be mopped up by thick hunks of crusty bread. It's a triumph. We only wish we'd thought of it first…

INGREDIENTS

900g mussels

1 tbsp olive oil

3 shallots, finely chopped

2 garlic cloves, crushed

1 red chilli, deseeded and finely chopped

425g good-quality tinned chopped tomatoes

300ml red wine

1 tbsp sun-dried tomato paste

Crusty bread, to serve

● Wash the mussels in cold water and discard any that do not close when tapped.

● In a large pan, heat the olive oil. Add the shallots, cover and cook over a low heat for 4–5 minutes until soft. Stir in the garlic and chilli, and cook for a further 30 seconds.

● Stir in the tinned tomatoes with their juice, red wine and sun-dried tomato paste. Bring to the boil, season with freshly ground black pepper and simmer for 15–20 minutes.

● Add the mussels to the pan. Cover with a lid and cook for 2–3 minutes or until all the mussels have opened. Discard any that remain closed.

● Ladle into serving bowls and serve straightaway with crusty bread.

THE HIVE
BREAKFAST BAP

SERVES 1

On Boxing Day and New Year's Day, you'll only find a selection of breakfast baps on The Hive menu. We sell around 500 each day; a huge proportion of which are our legendary bacon, sausage and egg baps – known in the kitchen as The BSE – which is just about the best cure for a hangover we know. Whenever possible, we use bacon from Dorset pigs, the pork sausages are made by our local butcher and the free-range eggs are brought in from farms across the county. Try sourcing your ingredients as locally as possible, too. You'll certainly taste the difference.

INGREDIENTS

Splash sunflower oil, for frying

3 chunky pork sausages

3 rashers good, thick-cut bacon

1 egg

1 bap

● Preheat your grill and pour sunflower oil into a frying pan ready to cook the eggs.

● Grill the sausages till they're golden-brown on all sides. Once cooked through, put them aside in a warm place.

● Next, grill the bacon to your liking. While you're doing this, put the frying pan on a low heat and crack an egg into the oil. Make sure you splash some hot oil over the top of the egg to fry it evenly.

● Slice open your bap and pile on the sausages, bacon and – finally – the egg. Enjoy with a steaming mug of tea.

ROAST POLLOCK IN A SHELLFISH STEW

SERVES 2

A wonderful winter warmer, this recipe is packed with some seriously stunning flavours. The mussels, king prawns, langoustines and clams in the stew provide a wonderfully robust base for the more delicate-tasting pollock fillets, and the result is a dish that showcases the very best the Dorset coast has to offer at this time of year. Here at The Hive, we're big believers in 'shell on', and the stew will taste better if the cases are left in. But if you're not keen on getting your fingers messy, feel free to use pre-peeled shellfish.

INGREDIENTS

8 mussels
8 clams
Butter
2 shallots, sliced
1 garlic clove, sliced
1 small glass white wine
400g good-quality tinned plum tomatoes
Handful parsley, chopped

Handful basil, chopped
Pinch saffron
1 lemon, juiced
2 200g pollock fillets
Olive oil
4 langoustines
2 king prawns

● Preheat your oven to 180°C/350°F. Wash the mussels and clams in cold water, and discard any that do not close when tapped.
● Warm a frying pan and put in a knob of butter. Cook the shallots and garlic until soft, then add the white wine, tomatoes, parsley, basil, saffron and lemon juice, and bring to the boil. Simmer gently for 5–10 minutes.
● Place the pollock fillets onto a roasting tray, then drizzle with olive oil and season. Roast for 10–15 minutes, until cooked through.
● While the fish is cooking, put all the shellfish into the pan, then cover and cook gently for around 10 minutes, until all the mussels and clams have opened, and the langoustines and prawns are cooked through. Discard any mussels or clams that remain closed, and set the stew aside in a warm place.
● Divide the shellfish stew between two large bowls and place a roasted pollock fillet on top of each. Serve immediately.

SEAFOOD SOUP

SERVES 2

The Hive's most famous dish, our seafood soup has been on the menu since Day One, and it's every bit as popular with our customers today as it was back then – especially when the weather is cold outside and they've just completed a long, blustery walk along the beach. As winter warmers go, this delicious combination of fresh and smoked fish, tomatoes and herbs, served with warm crusty bread, simply can't be beaten. People have come from far and wide to sample it, and will – we're sure – continue to do so for years to come.

INGREDIENTS

1 onion, finely sliced
1 stick celery, finely sliced
Butter
Olive oil
1 tsp dried thyme
1 tsp dried oregano
3 bay leaves

1 tbsp tomato purée
400g good-quality tinned chopped tomatoes
Small pinch cayenne pepper
250g mixed fish (at The Hive, we use
coley, smoked haddock and salmon),
roughly chopped

● Sweat the onion and celery in a large pan with a knob of butter and a drizzle of olive oil until soft. Add the thyme, oregano and bay leaves and cook for around 1 minute.
● Put in the tomato purée and cook for another couple of minutes, then pour in the tomatoes and cayenne pepper (feel free to add another pinch or two if you like your soup spicy), and bring up to a gentle simmer.
● Add the mixed fish to the pan and bring it back to a simmer, until the fish has cooked through. If the soup is too thick, simply add a little water.
● Check for seasoning, then serve hot with plenty of warm crusty bread.

ROASTED TURBOT STEAK IN A WILD MUSHROOM SAUCE

SERVES 2

Turbot – the king of the sea – may be expensive, but the financial outlay is worth it. And this recipe, which teams its firm, white flesh and deliciously subtle flavour with the earthy taste of wild mushrooms, fondant potatoes and confit of garlic, shows it at its best.

INGREDIENTS

1 garlic bulb, outer layers removed and sliced in half
Olive oil
2 Maris Piper potatoes
Clarified butter
2 250g turbot steaks
Butter

2 handfuls wild mushrooms
Splash white wine
150ml chicken stock
Splash double cream
2 sprigs thyme
Handful parsley, chopped

● Preheat your oven to 180°C/350°F. In a pan, immerse the two halves of the garlic bulb in olive oil and cook over a very low heat for up to 40 minutes, until the garlic is soft.

● Peel and barrel the potatoes (a perfect barrel shape isn't necessary, but it is essential that both potatoes are the same size so they require the same cooking time). Coat them in clarified butter and bake in the oven for around 15 minutes, until they are fluffy in the middle. Turn occasionally, and coat with more clarified butter if they look dry.

● Coat the turbot steaks in olive oil and sea salt, and place on a roasting tray. Roast for around 15 minutes, until cooked through.

● While the fish is cooking, warm a frying pan. When it's hot, drizzle in some olive oil and add a knob of butter, then sauté the wild mushrooms until they're golden-brown. Add the white wine and reduce; pour in the chicken stock and reduce by half. Put in the cream and reduce further until the sauce has a lovely, thick consistency.

● Put a turbot steak onto each plate and coat with the wild-mushroom sauce. Place a fondant potato on the side, and top with a confit of garlic, a sprig of thyme and the chopped parsley. Serve immediately.

OYSTERS
THREE WAYS

ALL RECIPES SERVE 2

Oysters may be delicious served raw – accompanied with Tabasco and a squeeze of lemon juice – but they're equally fabulous cooked. These three simple and quick recipes offer a wonderful variety of textures and flavours.

OYSTERS KILPATRICK

INGREDIENTS

2 oysters

3 rashers bacon, cut into lardons

Butter

Olive oil

2 tbsp breadcrumbs

1 tbsp Worcestershire sauce

4 tbsp double cream

- Preheat your grill. Prepare the oysters according to the instructions on page 14, ensuring you retain the shells.
- Fry the bacon with a knob of butter and a splash of olive oil. Once crisp, add the breadcrumbs and cook until golden. Pour in the Worcestershire sauce and cream, and bring to the boil.
- Place the oysters back in their shells, cover in the mixture and grill until golden.

TEMPURA OYSTERS

INGREDIENTS

Sunflower oil, for deep-frying

2 handfuls plain flour

Splash sparkling water

Sprig parsley, chopped

½ tsp poppy seeds

½ tsp sesame seeds

2 oysters

- Heat a pan of sunflower oil (or a deep-fat fryer) to around 180°C/350°F.
- Mix together 1 handful of flour and the sparkling water to create a thin batter. Add the parsley, poppy and sesame seeds, and season with a pinch of sea salt. Set aside.
- Prepare the oysters according to the instructions on page 14, ensuring you retain the shells. Roll the oysters in the remaining flour, then coat in batter. Deep-fry until crisp.

GIN & LIME OYSTERS

INGREDIENTS

2 oysters

Splash gin

Tiny piece ginger, grated

Small pinch sugar

½ red chilli, chopped

1 lime, juiced and zested

- Prepare the oysters according to the instructions on page 14, ensuring you retain the shells. Put the gin, ginger, sugar, chilli, and lime juice and zest into a bowl. Mix well.
- Place the oysters back in their shells and pour a spoonful of the gin-and-lime mixture over the top of each. Serve immediately.

SMOKED HADDOCK RISOTTO FISHCAKES

SERVES 2

A stunning combination of salty haddock flakes and creamy risotto in a deliciously crisp coating, this warming dish is best served with a large dollop of homemade Hollandaise sauce. An equally large glass of white wine on the side goes very well too…

INGREDIENTS

2 naturally smoked haddock fillets, skinned and pin-boned

500ml fish stock (see page 15)

Butter

1 onion, finely diced

1 stick celery, finely sliced

1 garlic clove, crushed

200g Arborio rice

Glass white wine

Handful parsley, chopped

Handful dill, chopped

1 lemon, juiced

Sunflower oil, for deep-frying

2 handfuls plain flour

Dash white wine vinegar

2 eggs

Homemade Hollandaise sauce (see page 16)

● Put the smoked haddock in an oven-proof dish and add enough fish stock to cover. Bring to the boil, then cover and simmer for 5 minutes, until cooked through. Leave to cool, then remove the fish and set aside. Retain the fish stock.

● Melt a knob of butter in a pan and sweat the onion, celery and garlic until soft, then add the Arborio rice and cook for around 1 minute. Pour in the white wine and reduce by half, then add the reserved fish stock in stages, stirring regularly and waiting until the rice has absorbed it before adding more. Once all the stock has gone in, remove from the heat.

● Stir the cooked smoked haddock, parsley and dill into the rice mixture, then add lemon juice and seasoning. Leave to cool and then shape into 4 tennis ball-sized fishcakes.

● Preheat the sunflower oil to 180°C/350°F in a large pan or deep-fat fryer. Roll the fishcakes in seasoned flour until fully covered, then deep-fry until golden-brown and piping-hot throughout.

● Bring a pan of water, the white wine vinegar and a pinch of sea salt up to the boil, then reduce to a gentle simmer. Crack in the eggs and soft-poach them for 3–4 minutes until they hold their shape while the yolks remain runny.

● Serve the fishcakes with the poached eggs and a drizzle of Hollandaise sauce on top.

SCALLOPS IN A CREAMY LEEK & SAFFRON SAUCE

SERVES 2

Here at The Hive, we always garnish this dish – a stunning combination of delicate Lyme Bay scallops and creamy leeks with a salty pancetta edge – with micro herbs, as they provide an intense burst of flavour. Don't worry if you don't have any to hand, though; watercress or rocket make perfectly acceptable substitutes. You must, however, include leeks, as they're at their very best during winter and spring, and are the perfect complement to seafood. Indeed, this delicious sauce works just as well with most grilled or fried fillets of fish.

INGREDIENTS

Butter
2 leeks, chopped
Pinch saffron
Splash white wine
Splash chicken stock
Glass double cream

4 slices pancetta
12 scallops
Olive oil
Baby basil leaves, to garnish
Baby coriander leaves, to garnish

● Preheat your grill. Melt a knob of butter in a saucepan and sweat the leeks until soft.
● Add the saffron and cook for 1 minute, then pour in the white wine and reduce by half. Add in the chicken stock and reduce by half again, then pour in the cream and reduce the sauce until it reaches a thick consistency. Set aside in a warm place.
● Arrange the pancetta slices on a baking tray and grill until crisp. Remove from under the heat and set aside in a warm place.
● Preheat a frying pan. Coat the scallops in olive oil and season, then add them to the pan. Fry on each side for 1 minute, until the flesh turns golden-brown. When the scallops are coloured all over, remove the pan from the heat and set aside.
● Divide the sauce between 2 plates and place the scallops on top. Arrange the crispy pancetta over these and finish with the baby basil and coriander leaves. Serve immediately.

SALMON & WILD MUSHROOMS IN A PUFF PASTRY PARCEL

SERVES 2

A great meal for special occasions, this dish seals the moistness and succulent flavour of salmon inside a puff pastry case and releases it only when it reaches your mouth. Time-poor party hosts will be glad to know it can be made up to 24 hours in advance, and kept in the fridge overnight before baking. Serve it as we do on winter afternoons at The Hive, with new potatoes and vegetables, and slathered in a wonderfully creamy white wine sauce.

INGREDIENTS

Butter

1 leek, finely chopped

Handful wild mushrooms

Sprig parsley, chopped

Plain flour, for rolling

1 puff pastry sheet

2 175g salmon fillets

1 egg, beaten

Glass white wine

Glass fish stock (see page 15)

Glass double cream

Handful dill, chopped

● Preheat your oven to 180°C/350°F. Melt a knob of butter in a pan and sweat the leek until soft, then add the mushrooms and cook on a high heat until all the moisture has evaporated. Stir in the parsley then set aside in a warm place.

● Dust a clean work surface with flour and roll out the puff pastry sheet into a large square. Cut it in half, and place the leek-and-mushroom mixture into the centre of each rectangle. Arrange the salmon fillets on top.

● Fold the pastry around the filling and brush the outer edges with the beaten egg. Pinch the pastry together to completely seal in the salmon, and rest in the fridge for at least 30 minutes before cooking.

● To cook the parcels, place them on a buttered baking sheet and brush all over with beaten egg. Bake for around 30 minutes, until golden-brown and cooked through.

● While the parcels are cooking, prepare the sauce. Pour the white wine into a pan and reduce by half, then add the fish stock and reduce by half again. Pour in the cream and reduce the sauce until it reaches a thick consistency. Season, finish with dill and serve while hot.

OUR SUPPLIERS: DAVY'S LOCKER, BRIDPORT

'If it comes out of the sea and somebody wants it, we'll try and get it,' says Paul Wickham (*left*) of Bridport seafood retailer and wholesaler Davy's Locker. 'We buy from our local fish market at Brixham; we've got a couple of guys who fish in West Bay for us; and we buy fish from as far afield as Peterhead, Fraserburgh, Grimsby and Aberdeen. We persevere to keep the standard as high as we can.

'How do we maintain the quality? Easy. If it isn't good enough, it goes back to whoever has delivered it. Our customers don't receive it. We'd rather say no than send out something horrible. I don't think the public realise that a fish on a counter could be a fortnight old before it even gets to the shore. That's why we buy from day boats. I'm also a great fan of static netting rather than trawling because the fish swim into it. You don't catch the fish; the fish commit suicide.

'Dave Park, who started the company, used to go down to Looe with his dad to the fish markets, and that's how Davy's Locker began. He operated out of his garage at the other end of Bridport. Back then, we supplied local restaurants and hotels, just as we do now, but as our customers have grown, we've grown with them. And we tend to pick up new ones through word of mouth. We don't advertise at all. It's down to customer service; we don't tell lies and we always do what we say we're going to do.

'One major restaurant customer – not The Hive, I should say – phoned us up and said, "can you get us a large halibut?". I asked around and Grimsby came up with one that weighed 130 kilos. The chef rang me back a couple of days later and asked if I'd found one. I said, "yeah, 130 kilos. It's here now." He went "How big? Bloody hell. What are we going to tell the boss!?" And, no word of a lie, it took five of us to carry the bugger in. There was a picture of us in *The Times* trying to get it through the door.'

Davy's Locker, Dreadnought Trading Estate, Bridport (01308 456131; www.davyslocker.co.uk).

MUSSELS IN A RED THAI BROTH

SERVES 2

The clean, fresh flavours of Thai food are perfectly at home in the cold British winter, and the aromatic spices and heat in this delicious broth sit as naturally with Lyme Bay mussels at The Hive as they would with any giga or gar in the beachside cafés of Phuket or Koh Phi Phi. You can alter the fieriness of this dish by simply adding or subtracting the number of red chillies in the recipe, but we recommend you serve it lip-searingly hot.

INGREDIENTS

900g mussels

Splash sesame oil

1 onion, diced

2 garlic cloves, crushed

2 red chillies, finely chopped

1 thumb-sized ginger root, grated

1 tbsp Thai red curry paste

400g tinned coconut milk

Splash Thai Nam Pla fish sauce

1 lime, zested and juiced

1 tbsp brown sugar

2 kaffir lime leaves, shredded

2 sticks lemongrass, white part chopped

Handful coriander, chopped

10 Thai basil leaves, shredded

● Wash the mussels in cold water and discard any that do not close when tapped.

● Heat the sesame oil in a pan and sweat the onion until soft. Add the garlic, chillies, ginger and Thai red curry paste, and cook for around 1 minute.

● Put the mussels into the pan and cook for a further minute, then add the coconut milk, Thai Nam Pla fish sauce, lime zest and juice, sugar, kaffir lime leaves and lemongrass. Cover and cook for 2–3 minutes over a high heat, until the mussels have opened. Discard any that remain closed.

● Sprinkle with coriander and Thai basil leaves, and serve immediately.

Goldfish BM4
Pollock Line 2 2x35
70.00 kg

TEMPURA POLLOCK IN A CREAMY LEEK & SAFFRON SAUCE

SERVES 2

This saucy take on fish and chips is one of the most popular dishes on The Hive's winter menu, and the freshness of its ingredients combine to create something rather special. Leeks are in their prime at this time of year and pollock – a cheaper and far more sustainable alternative to cod – is plentiful off the Dorset coast.

INGREDIENTS

Sunflower oil, for deep-frying
3 cups plain flour
150ml sparkling water
Handful parsley, finely chopped
2 leeks, finely chopped
Butter

Pinch saffron
Glass white wine
Splash chicken stock
Splash double cream
2 260g pollock fillets, scaled and pin-boned
2 handfuls watercress, washed

● Preheat the sunflower oil to 180°C/350°F in a large pan or deep-fat fryer.

● Whisk together 2 cups of flour with the sparkling water to create a thin batter. Mix in the chopped parsley and set aside.

● Sweat the leeks with a knob of butter until soft, then add the saffron and cook for 1 minute. Pour in the white wine and reduce by half, then add the chicken stock and reduce by half again. Pour in the cream and reduce until the sauce has a lovely, thick consistency. Set aside in a warm place.

● Spread out the remaining flour and plenty of sea salt on a baking tray, and coat the pollock fillets thoroughly with the mixture. Dip the fillets into the batter, ensuring they are fully covered, and deep-fry for 8–10 minutes, until the batter is golden and the fish has cooked through.

● Divide the creamy saffron-and-leek sauce between 2 plates, and place a small handful of watercress on top. Arrange the battered fish fillets over this and serve immediately with hot bowls of chips.

LOBSTER THERMIDOR

SERVES 2

The rocks between Burton Bradstock and Freshwater Beach are the perfect hiding place for lobsters – until fisherman Steve Elsworth and his boat Dorado arrive on the scene, that is. Steve lands the majority of the lobsters we use in the café, and the flags that stand around 150 yards offshore from the Hive mark his pots. You can't, we think, get much more local than that. And the quality of his catch is shown off to perfection in our take on this classic recipe.

INGREDIENTS

2 live lobsters

2 shallots, diced

Splash white wine vinegar

100ml fish stock (see page 15)

50ml double cream

2 tsp English mustard

50g strong cheddar

2 egg yolks

Parmesan, grated

● Prepare and cook the lobsters according to the instructions on page 13. Once done, put them to one side to cool.

● For the thermidor sauce, put the shallots in a pan with the white wine vinegar and reduce by half.

● Add the fish stock and reduce the mixture till almost all of the liquid has evaporated, then put in two-thirds of the cream and reduce once again. Add in the mustard and cheddar, and leave to cool.

● Cut the cooled lobsters in half and remove the tail meat. Retain the shells and chop the tail meat into chunks.

● Whisk the egg yolks and add to the thermidor sauce. Then whisk up the remaining cream and stir that in as well. Mix in the chopped lobster.

● Spoon the thermidor mixture back into the lobster shells, grate over some parmesan and grill until golden-brown and hot throughout.

BOUILLABAISSE

SERVES 4

This delicious, thick seafood stew – our version of the Provençal classic – is dished up in great quantities at The Hive during the winter months. We always use red mullet because it adds great colour and flavour, but this recipe is here simply as a guide – feel free to experiment with whatever fish and shellfish you can get your hands on. Bouillabaisse is ideal for serving to large groups as not only is it incredibly easy to make, but it also looks and smells amazing. Serve it in the pan in which it's cooked and watch everyone dig in.

INGREDIENTS

20 mussels

1kg red mullet, monkfish and seabass fillets, scaled and pin-boned

Butter

1 onion, finely chopped

1 fennel bulb, finely chopped

3 bay leaves

1 sprig parsley

1 sprig thyme

Pinch saffron

750g tomatoes, peeled and chopped

500ml fish stock (see page 15)

Handful chives, chopped

Homemade rouille (see page 17)

● Wash the mussels in cold water and discard any that do not close when tapped. Cut the red mullet, monkfish and seabass into chunks.

● Melt a knob of butter in a pan and sweat the onion and fennel for around 5 minutes, until soft. Add the bay leaves, parsley, thyme, saffron, tomatoes and fish stock, and boil for 10 minutes. If you prefer a smooth bouillabaisse (we don't at The Hive), you can sieve the liquid at this point.

● Add the fish and mussels, then cover and simmer until the fish has cooked through and all the mussels have opened. Discard any that remain closed.

● Sprinkle with chives, then serve straight from the pan with homemade rouille and hot, crusty bread on the side.

MACKEREL FILLETS WITH CELERIAC REMOULADE

SERVES 2

The sharp, aniseedy flavour of celeriac makes it the perfect accompaniment to many a dish – we often serve it as a remoulade at The Hive with slices of Parma or Serrano ham – but it works exceptionally well with the strong, robust and oily meat in freshly caught mackerel. These beautiful fish are plentiful off the Dorset coast throughout autumn and winter, and their glistening, silvery flesh is as gorgeous to eat as it is to look at.

INGREDIENTS

½ celeriac, peeled and grated

1 lemon, juiced

1 tbsp Dijon mustard

Handful flat-leaf parsley, chopped

Mayonnaise (see page 16)

4 mackerel, divided into 8 fillets

Olive oil

● To create the remoulade, place the celeriac, lemon juice, mustard and parsley into a large bowl, along with sea salt and freshly ground black pepper. Mix well and stir in the homemade mayonnaise. Season to taste and set aside.

● Preheat your grill. Season the mackerel fillets with olive oil and sea salt.

● Put the mackerel fillets onto a baking tray, skin side up, and place under a hot grill for 4–6 minutes, until cooked through.

● Divide the fillets between 2 plates and serve immediately with celeriac remoulade and lemon wedges on the side.

CRISPY SALT & PEPPER SQUID

SERVES 2

Squid is plentiful and relatively cheap in West Dorset, so it's something we use a lot of at The Hive. This nutritious dish is really quick to prepare, but it requires speedy serving to avoid the squid becoming too rubbery. The herbs and spices used in the crispy coating and the dipping mayonnaise aren't an exact science, so you should feel free to alter the measurements or even add in your own favourites according to taste.

INGREDIENTS

Homemade mayonnaise (see page 16)
150ml sweet chilli sauce
Handful chives, chopped
1 lemon, cut into 4 segments
Handful cornflour
Pinch paprika

Pinch cayenne pepper
400g cleaned squid, cut into tentacles
and rings
Sunflower oil, for deep-frying
Salad leaves

● First, take the homemade mayonnaise and stir in the sweet chilli sauce, chives and juice of 2 lemon segments. Spoon it into two ramekins and put to one side.
● Mix together the cornflour, paprika and cayenne pepper with some sea salt and freshly ground black pepper. Coat the squid pieces thoroughly with the mixture.
● Heat the sunflower oil to 180°C/350°F in a large pan or deep-fat fryer. While it's warming, arrange any salad you'd like as an accompaniment on two plates. You'll need to serve up quickly once the squid is ready.
● Once the oil is hot enough, drop in the squid tentacles. Deep-fry these for around a minute, then add the squid rings and cook for another couple of minutes, until crispy.
● Remove the squid pieces with a slotted spoon and place on a piece of kitchen towel to absorb the excess oil. Pile onto the plates and serve immediately with the chilli mayonnaise and remaining lemon segments.

OYSTERS WITH PANCETTA & CREAMY PARMESAN SAUCE

SERVES 2

Though most people prefer to eat their oysters cold, this delicious recipe is a great introduction to the delights of the hot bivalve. The crisp, salty pancetta perfectly complements the tender brininess of the oyster, and the creamy sauce is as good an antidote as any to the cold, gloomy days of winter. At The Hive, we always use oysters from the River Yealm in neighbouring Devon. But if you seek out oysters that are reared as closely to you as possible, there's no reason why your version of this dish won't taste every bit as good as ours.

INGREDIENTS

12 oysters
4 shallots, finely sliced
1 garlic clove, chopped
Butter
Olive oil

Splash white wine
Splash fish stock (see page 15)
600ml double cream
150g pancetta, cut into lardons
Parmesan, for grating

● Preheat your grill. Prepare the oysters according to the instructions on page 14, ensuring you retain the shells.
● Pan-fry the shallots and garlic with a knob of butter and a drizzle of olive oil, until the shallots are soft. Add the white wine and fish stock and reduce by half; pour in the cream and reduce by half again. Set aside in a warm place.
● Melt a knob of butter in a pan and fry the pancetta until crisp. Add the pancetta to the cream sauce.
● Place the oysters back in their shells, cover with the cream sauce and finish with grated parmesan. Grill until golden-brown.
● Serve immediately with warm crusty bread and a chilled bottle of Champagne.

INDEX

A

aïoli: baked turbot steak with saffron aïoli **52**
anchovies: lemon sole with anchovy & herb butter **86**; seabass Niçoise **116**; mackerel with new potatoes & tapenade **160**; cuttlefish stew **166**
asparagus: smoked haddock with asparagus benedict **64**
avocado: Weymouth crab & avocado salad **94**; whiting goujons with guacamole **198**

B

bacon: monkfish in streaky bacon **40**; smoked haddock chowder **182**; The Hive breakfast bap **216**; oysters three ways **226**
beetroot: smoked mackerel with horseradish crème fraîche **68**
black bream: chargrilled black bream with lemon & rosemary **98**
blackeyed beans: turbot with blackeyed bean cassoulet **176**
boudin noir (black pudding): scallops with boudin noir & pea purée **148**
brandy: homecured gravlax **152**; lobster bisque **154**; hot shellfish risotto **194**
brill: brill with sautéed wild mushrooms **140**; tempura brill with a creamy pancetta sauce **188**; brill with a poached duck's egg & pancetta **206**
butter beans: seafood, tomato & chorizo broth **28**
butternut squash: baked pouting in a curried mussel broth **196**

C

cabbage: roasted cod with buttered cabbage, pancetta & tomato **202**
capers: scallops in a beurre noisette **44**; skate wing with brown butter & caper sauce **124**; Dover sole with a shrimp & caper butter **136**; mackerel with new potatoes & tapenade **160**; cuttlefish stew **166**
celeriac: mackerel fillets with celeriac remoulade **244**
cheese: spiced spider crab gratin **74**;

smoked haddock rarebit with roasted tomatoes **168**; red mullet with homemade pesto **170**; The Hive fish pie **200**; baked scallops in a cheese sauce **204**; lobster thermidor **240**; oysters with pancetta & creamy parmesan sauce **248**
chilli: Lesley Waters' hot & sour prawn soup **58**; hake with chilli & tomato chutney **96**; squid with a chilli, coriander & lime butter **118**; chilli crab linguine **172**; whiting goujons with guacamole & chilli salt **198**; The Hive hot shellfish platter **210**; smoked haddock kedgeree **212**; Lesley Waters' garlic mussel bisque **214**; oysters three ways **226**; mussels in a red Thai broth **236**
chilli sauce: crevette prawns in a sweet & sticky chilli sauce **150**; crispy salt & pepper squid **246**
Chinese five spice: pan-fried huss with Chinese five spice **156**
chorizo: seafood, tomato & chorizo broth **28**; Hive hash **50**; seared scallops with pancetta & chorizo **110**; turbot with blackeyed bean cassoulet **176**
cider: razor clams with cider, leeks & parsley **32**; John Dory in a cockle, baby leek & cider broth **70**
clams: surf clam chowder **142**; The Hive hot shellfish platter **210**; roast pollock in a shellfish stew **218**
cockles: John Dory in a cockle, baby leek & cider broth **70**
coconut milk: mussels in a red Thai broth **236**
cod: The Hive ultimate fish burger **26**; seafood, tomato & chorizo broth **28**; baked cod with a herb crust **34**; tempura cod with minted mushy peas **102**; The Hive fish pie **200**; roasted cod with buttered cabbage, pancetta & tomato **202**
coley: seafood, tomato & chorizo broth **28**; seafood soup **222**
crab: grey mullet with crab & Jersey royal salad **56**; spiced spider crab gratin **74**; Hive cold shellfish platter **80**; Weymouth crab &

avocado salad **94**; Burton Bradstock brown crab salad **122**; chilli crab linguine **172**
crayfish: baked plaice with crayfish & herb butter **128**
crème fraîche: grilled herrings with horseradish crème fraîche **20**; seafood, tomato & chorizo broth **28**; smoked mackerel with horseradish crème fraîche **68**
curly kale: sea trout with curly kale bubble & squeak **60**
cuttlefish: cuttlefish stew **166**

D

dab: dabs with lemon & garlic butter **112**
Dover sole: Dover sole in parsley & garlic butter **100**; Dover sole with a shrimp & caper butter **136**

F

French beans: seabass Niçoise **116**; Lesley Waters' rainbow trout fishcakes **174**

G

garfish: grilled garfish with lemon zest, parsley & olive oil **190**
gin: oysters three ways **226**
ginger: hake with chilli & tomato chutney **96**; Lesley Waters' hot & sour prawn soup **58**; smoked haddock kedgeree **212**; oysters three ways **226**; mussels in a red Thai broth **236**
grey mullet: grey mullet with crab & Jersey royal salad **56**
Guinness: oysters & Guinness **186**
gurnard: roasted gurnard with olive oil & sea salt **85**

H

haddock: seafood, tomato & chorizo broth **28**; smoked haddock with asparagus benedict **64**; smoked haddock rarebit with roasted tomatoes **168**; smoked haddock chowder **182**; smoked haddock kedgeree **212**; seafood soup **222**; smoked haddock risotto fishcakes **228**
hake: hake with sautéed spring greens **54**; hake with chilli & tomato chutney **96**
halibut: halibut with mussels & saffron cream sauce **48**; baked halibut steaks with a hazelnut crust **164**

hazelnuts: baked halibut steaks with a hazelnut crust **164**
herring: grilled herrings with horseradish crème fraîche **20**; kippers & soft poached eggs on granary toast **184**
herring roe: tempura herring roe salad **144**
horseradish: grilled herrings with horseradish crème fraîche **20**; smoked mackerel with horseradish crème fraîche **68**
huss: huss fishfingers with tartare sauce **126**; huss with Chinese five spice **156**

J

John Dory: John Dory with crispy leeks & a mustard sauce **42**; John Dory in a cockle, baby leek & cider broth **70**; baked John Dory with rosemary & cherry tomatoes **78**

K

kippers: kippers & soft poached eggs on granary toast **184**

L

langoustines: langoustines with spring pea risotto **22**; The Hive cold shellfish platter **80**; hot shellfish risotto **194**; The Hive hot shellfish platter **210**; roast pollock in a shellfish stew **218**
leeks: turbot with baby leeks & cava cream sauce **24**; seafood, tomato & chorizo broth **28**; razor clams with cider, leeks & parsley **32**; John Dory with crispy leeks & a mustard sauce **42**; halibut with mussels & saffron cream sauce **48**; John Dory in a cockle, baby leek & cider broth **70**; surf clam chowder **142**; smoked haddock chowder **182**; scallops in a creamy leek & saffron sauce **230**; salmon & wild mushrooms in a puff pastry parcel **232**; tempura pollock in a creamy leek & saffron sauce **238**
lemon sole: lemon sole with anchovy & herb butter **86**; Lesley Waters' glazed lemon sole tart **130**
lettuce: The Hive ultimate fish burger **26**; roasted hake with sautéed spring greens **54**
lobster: The Hive cold shellfish platter **80**; grilled lobster with garlic butter **104**; lobster bisque **154**; hot shellfish risotto **194**; The Hive hot shellfish platter **210**; lobster thermidor **240**

M

mackerel: chargrilled mackerel with salsa verde **36**; smoked mackerel with horseradish crème fraîche **68**; mackerel with red onion & red pepper salsa **88**; mackerel with new potatoes & tapenade **160**; mackerel fillets with celeriac remoulade **244**

monkfish: monkfish in streaky bacon **40**; bouillabaisse **242**

mushrooms: Hive hash **50**; brill with sautéed wild mushrooms **140**; roasted turbot steak in a wild mushroom sauce **224**; salmon & wild mushrooms in a puff pastry parcel **232**

mussels: seafood, tomato & chorizo broth **28**; halibut with mussels & saffron sauce **48**; mussels with white wine, herbs, garlic & cream **90**; mussels in a red wine, thyme & tomato sauce **158**; hot shellfish risotto **194**; baked pouting in a curried mussel broth **196**; The Hive hot shellfish platter **210**; Lesley Waters' garlic mussel bisque **214**; roast pollock in a shellfish stew **218**; mussels in a red Thai broth **236**; bouillabaisse **242**

N

noodles: Lesley Waters' hot & sour prawn soup **58**

O

olives: sardines on toast Neapolitan **72**; mackerel with new potatoes & tapenade **160**

oysters: The Hive cold shellfish platter **80**; oysters Rockefeller **138**; oysters & Guinness **186**; oysters three ways **226**; oysters with pancetta & creamy parmesan sauce **248**

P

pancetta: seafood, tomato & chorizo broth **28**; Hive hash **50**; seared scallops with pancetta & chorizo **110**; surf clam chowder **142**; tempura brill with a creamy pancetta sauce **188**; roasted cod with buttered cabbage, pancetta & tomato **202**; scallops in a creamy leek & saffron sauce **230**; brill with duck's egg & pancetta **206**; oysters with pancetta & creamy parmesan sauce **248**

pasta: chilli crab linguine **172**

peas: langoustines with spring pea risotto **22**; roasted hake with sautéed spring greens **54**; plaice goujons with minted

mushy peas **82**; tempura cod with minted mushy peas **102**; scallops with boudin noir & pea purée **148**; tempura brill with a creamy pancetta sauce **188**

pine nuts: red mullet with homemade pesto **170**

plaice: plaice goujons with minted mushy peas **82**; baked plaice with crayfish & herb butter **128**

pollock: roast pollock in a shellfish stew **218**; tempura pollock in a creamy leek & saffron sauce **238**

potatoes: langoustines with spring pea risotto **22**; Hive hash **50**; grey mullet with crab & Jersey royal salad **56**; sea trout with curly kale bubble & squeak **60**; smoked mackerel with horseradish crème fraîche **68**; seabass Niçoise **116**; surf clam chowder **142**; mackerel with new potatoes & tapenade **160**; Lesley Waters' rainbow trout fishcakes **174**; smoked haddock chowder **182**; The Hive fish pie **200**; baked scallops in a cheese sauce **204**; roasted turbot steak in a wild mushroom sauce **224**

pouting: baked pouting in a curried mussel broth **196**

prawns: seafood, tomato & chorizo broth **28**; Lesley Waters' hot & sour prawn soup **58**; The Hive cold shellfish platter **80**; crevette prawns in a sweet & sticky chilli sauce **150**; hot shellfish risotto **194**; The Hive hot shellfish platter **210**; roast pollock in a shellfish stew **218**

R

rainbow trout: Lesley Waters' rainbow trout fishcakes **174**

razor clams: razor clams with cider, leeks & parsley **32**; razor clams with a lemon & lime vinaigrette **180**

red mullet: red mullet with homemade pesto **170**; bouillabaisse **242**

rice: langoustines with spring pea risotto **22**; hot shellfish risotto **194**; smoked haddock kedgeree **212**; smoked haddock risotto fishcakes **228**

S

saffron: halibut with mussels & saffron cream sauce **48**; baked turbot steak with saffron aïoli **52**; cuttlefish stew **166**; hot shellfish risotto **194**; baked pouting in a curried mussel broth **196**; roast pollock in a shellfish stew **218**; scallops in a creamy leek & saffron sauce **230**; tempura pollock in a creamy leek & saffron sauce **238**; bouillabaisse **242**

salmon: seared salmon with buttered spinach **39**; smoked salmon & scrambled eggs **114**; homecured gravlax **152**; The Hive fish pie **200**; seafood soup **222**; salmon & wild mushrooms in a puff pastry parcel **232**

salsa: chargrilled mackerel with salsa verde **36**; mackerel with red onion & red pepper salsa **88**; Lesley Waters' rainbow trout fishcakes **174**

samphire: hake with chilli & tomato chutney **96**

sardines: sardines on toast Neapolitan **72**; peppered sardines with sea salt **132**

sausages: The Hive breakfast bap **216**

scallops: scallops in a beurre noisette **44**; scallop scampi with homemade tartare sauce **66**; seared scallops with pancetta & chorizo **110**; scallops with boudin noir & pea purée **148**; hot shellfish risotto **194**; baked scallops in a cheese sauce **204**; scallops in a creamy leek & saffron sauce **230**

scampi: scallop scampi with homemade tartare sauce **66**

seabass: seabass for two **106**; seabass Niçoise **116**; bouillabaisse **242**

sea trout: sea trout with curly kale bubble & squeak **60**

shrimps: Dover sole with a shrimp & caper butter **136**

skate: skate wing with brown butter & caper sauce **124**

spinach: seared salmon with buttered spinach **39**; Lesley Waters' rainbow trout fishcakes **174**

squid: seafood, tomato & chorizo broth **28**; squid with a chilli, coriander & lime butter **118**; crispy salt & pepper squid **246**

sugar snap peas: Lesley Waters' hot & sour prawn soup **58**

sweetcorn: smoked haddock chowder **182**;

sweet potatoes: baked pouting in a curried mussel broth **196**

T

tomatoes: seafood, tomato & chorizo broth **28**; monkfish in streaky bacon **40**; sardines on toast Neapolitan **72**; baked John Dory with rosemary & cherry tomatoes **78**; Weymouth crab & avocado salad **94**; hake with chilli & tomato chutney **96**; lobster bisque **154**; mussels in a red wine, thyme & tomato sauce **158**; cuttlefish stew **166**; smoked haddock rarebit with roasted tomatoes **168**; turbot with blackeyed bean cassoulet **176**; hot shellfish risotto **194**; roasted cod with buttered cabbage, pancetta & tomato **202**; Lesley Waters' garlic mussel bisque **214**; roast pollock in a shellfish stew **218**; seafood soup **222**; bouillabaisse **242**

turbot: turbot with baby leeks & cava cream sauce **24**; baked turbot steak with saffron aïoli **52**; turbot with blackeyed bean cassoulet **176**; roasted turbot steak in a wild mushroom sauce **224**

W

whiting: whiting goujons with guacamole & chilli salt **198**

wine: langoustines with spring pea risotto **22**; turbot with baby leeks & cava cream **24**; baked cod with a herb crust **34**; halibut with mussels & saffron cream sauce **48**; sardines on toast Neapolitan **72**; mussels with white wine, herbs, garlic & cream **90**; brill with sautéed wild mushrooms **140**; surf clam chowder **142**; crevette prawns in a sweet & sticky chilli sauce **150**; lobster bisque **154**; mussels in a red wine, thyme & tomato sauce **158**; cuttlefish stew **166**; smoked haddock chowder **182**; tempura brill with a creamy pancetta sauce **188**; baked pouting in a curried mussel broth **196**; The Hive hot shellfish platter **210**; Lesley Waters' garlic mussel bisque **214**; roast pollock in a shellfish stew **218**; roasted turbot steak in a wild mushroom sauce **224**; smoked haddock risotto fishcakes **228**; scallops in a creamy leek & saffron sauce **230**; salmon & wild mushrooms in a puff pastry parcel **232**; tempura pollock in a creamy leek & saffron sauce **238**; oysters with pancetta & creamy parmesan sauce **248**

THANK YOU

THE HIVE BEACH CAFÉ WOULD LIKE TO THANK...

Steve Attrill for allowing his staff the time and freedom to prepare, trial, cook and photograph the dishes in this book; **Debbie Attrill** for her endless patience, and the use of tablecloths and other props; and **Lesley Waters** for her ongoing support of The Hive and its chefs.

Huge thanks, too, to **Melanie Attrill**, **Janet Hallbery**, **Toman Lau**, **Cerian Henshaw**, **Tim Macpherson**, **Daniel Rushall**, **Annette Shaw** and, of course, **our loyal customers,** without whom none of this would have been possible.

BRISTLEBIRD BOOKS WOULD LIKE TO THANK...

Ginny Henry for her picture-editing brilliance; **Sarah Maber** for her support and constant stream of ideas; **Nigel Skeels** for his help with *The Hive Beach Café Cookbook* website; **Guy Staniforth** for his enormous contribution to this project, and for trusting us with his hard-earned money; and, finally, to **Bob and Judith Purdy** for their patience, support and all those cups of tea. We couldn't have done it without you.

THE HIVE BEACH CAFÉ, BEACH ROAD, BURTON BRADSTOCK, DORSET DT6 4RF

WWW.HIVEBEACHCAFE.CO.UK